FREEDOM
AND
LIBERTY

FREEDOM
AND
LIBERTY

BY

WILLIAM BENETT

Author of *The Ethical Aspects of Evolution*
Justice and Happiness, Religion and Freewill

OXFORD UNIVERSITY PRESS
LONDON   EDINBURGH   GLASGOW   NEW YORK
TORONTO   MELBOURNE   CAPE TOWN   BOMBAY
HUMPHREY MILFORD
1920

171.1
B465f

PREFACE

IN July 1916 I published an essay under the title of 'Freedom'. Its aim was purely ethical; that is, to show that, for the purposes of human evolution, each of the two opposites, law, or organic control, and liberty, or life, was of equal importance: that there can be no continued growth of the race as a whole without an equal growth of each of these conflicting principles. Beyond this conclusion I was unable to go. I recognized that as a system my philosophy was incomplete. It failed to provide the single final end without which the deduction of ethical values is impossible. But, at the time, I had little hope of carrying the inquiry further, and I published the results, as far as they went, in a cheap form, to preserve them from oblivion.

In my previous writings I had indicated that the universal final end of ethics must be found in religion, and there only. But what that final end is, in which of the many competing forms of religion it is to be found, and in what way it is to be connected with the contradictory judgements of ethics in such a way as to make a complete system, I had not discovered. An answer to these questions is attempted in the essay on 'Liberty', which has occupied me since the publication of the first essay, and is now finished.

The two essays are intimately connected, and are now bound together in one volume.

W. BENETT.

October 12, 1920.

CONTENTS

BOOK I. FREEDOM

		PAGE
I.	GENERAL PRINCIPLES	5
II.	PRACTICAL APPLICATIONS (with special reference to universal military service)	47
III.	INTERNATIONAL FREEDOM	89

BOOK II. LIBERTY

I.	MORALITY	109
II.	THE KINGDOM OF HEAVEN	169
III.	THE KINGDOM ON EARTH	221
IV.	FINAL ENDS, PHILOSOPHIC AND RELIGIOUS	297
V.	SUMMARY	337

BOOK I
FREEDOM

FREEDOM
GENERAL PRINCIPLES

Περὶ παντὸς τὴν ἐλευθερίαν

FREEDOM

Freedom is the watchword of England, and, through her, of all English-speaking peoples. The watchword of Rome was Law; of France, it is Liberty. Freedom combines the two contradictory principles of law and liberty. Neither of the subordinate principles is good by itself. Law ends in tyranny: liberty, in anarchy. From neither tyranny nor anarchy can any advancement of civilization be expected. Freedom, or the compromise between the two, in which neither has a decisive predominance, is the sole condition of progress. It is through freedom, and not by liberty alone, that 'human development in its richest diversity' can be realized. And this, as Wilhelm v. Humboldt remarks, in a passage prefixed by J. S. Mill to his essay 'On Liberty', is a matter of 'absolute and essential importance'. He might have gone farther. It is the sole and exclusive end of all ethical action which we call good.

This use of terms may be objected to as unusual and arbitrary. I can think of no other. There are three concepts to which words must be fitted. Those are the conflicting impulses of activity and restraint, and their amalgamation as restrained or organized activity; and the only words in our language which will serve our purpose are liberty, law, and freedom. Licence is an excess of liberty, as slavery is an excess of restraint, but liberty and licence are no more convertible terms than law and slavery are.

'Human development in its richest diversity' is nothing but a picturesque expression for the output of human activity in its greatest possible intensity and variety. A man, who, like Robinson Crusoe before his encounter with Friday, lived by himself on a desert island, must still be a law to himself, but, subject to that, he might exercise all his faculties to the utmost, and in any direction he chose. He would be subject to no external restraint. When, however, he is a member of a society, the centre of interest is transferred from the individual to the society; and the final end of action becomes the greatest output of power, not of himself, but of the whole community of which he is a member. In order to secure that object it is necessary that the activities of all and each of the members of the society should be co-ordinated and focussed in one direction, towards a common end.

The principle of direction and co-ordination is (in the widest sense of the word) law; and it is through law that a community becomes free, and capable of putting forth its maximum of power. Without law, it is incapable of putting forth any collective power whatever; and law is essentially the curtailment of the liberties of each individual member of the community. But the only justification for any retrenchment of individual liberty lies in the superior needs of the community as a whole; and when law carries its interference beyond that point the community ceases to be free.

The opposition between activity and restraint is universal, and extends to every branch of human conduct. Genius itself is unproductive unless it submits to rule. Where both are indispensable it is useless to ask which is the more valuable; but it is certain that, if they are to be distinguished as end and means, it is activity that must take the place of end. In political freedom we submit to law for the sake of liberty. To invert the terms, and say that we value liberty for the sake of law, would be a palpable absurdity. Nevertheless, to attribute the higher honour to law, so long as both are preserved, need not injure the cause of freedom. Rome, between the expulsion of the kings and the rise of the Empire, afforded the highest and most enduring example of political freedom the world had ever seen. That law should be preferred in honour is indeed desirable. The passion for liberty is so universal, and of such overwhelming strength, that no adventitious aid that may reinforce its opposite can safely be neglected. On the other hand, we may remember that law is an incident of evolution, and that if we care to push our speculations beyond the scheme of our present life, we can afford to dispense with the concept. We can, if we like, imagine an earthly Paradise, where every one gets, without effort, everything he wants. Or, in a higher vein, religion speaks to us of the perfect liberty of the regenerate. But those are regions in which no sober philosophy will venture to intrude.

There are two kinds of community of which freedom may be predicated. First, the community of discordant impulses which make up an individual. The co-ordination of these for the prosecution of a common end is moral freedom; and the greatest output of power is attained when the controlling principle is the conscience. In that case a man's aim is the development of his highest self. The second kind of community is the collection of individual men who make up a nation. A nation is free when the discordant interests of its members are co-ordinated in such a way as to secure the greatest possible output of force for the prosecution of the national end or ideal. The co-ordinating principle in political freedom is law, including public opinion of all kinds.

Personal Freedom

It is through the co-ordination of all the impulses of an individual by some internal rule or principle that his higher impulses are kept alive, and he becomes a reasonable man. That kind of co-ordination which provides for the satisfaction of the greatest possible volume and number of his conflicting impulses is freedom. Freedom is not itself the ultimate end of action, but it is the means, or necessary condition, of personal 'development in its richest diversity'. It is the condition which allows a man to maintain his present position in the scale of evolution, and to advance beyond it.

Moral freedom is the foundation of all other kinds of freedom. Every individual may be regarded as a republic of impulses to action, which are combined for the prosecution of a common end. Left to itself each several impulse must assert itself without regard to all the others. A state of things in which this could be realized might be described as perfect moral liberty. In practice it would be anarchy, or a war of all against all, in which the strongest must win. But the strongest impulse is, with most men, one of those in which he most nearly resembles the lower orders of creation. And degradation means loss of power, and eventual extinction. The man who is bound by no law, human or divine, is no longer a man but a monster.

Though it will be generally admitted that the conscience is, or ought to be, the supreme law for the guidance of human conduct, this is not the only answer that has been given to the problem, and a few words of explanation will not be superfluous. We may notice two others, in order to show on what grounds conscience deserves the preference, when the ends which are sought are those of freedom.

The first of these answers is that Religion gives the rules for right conduct. This is true in a sense, but, in the religion which we profess, the end is placed in another world, and it is gained by entry into a new life, in which all the ends of our life in this world are rejected as devoid of independent value.

With this aim freedom has no concern whatever. Its aims are confined to this world, and do not look beyond it. The aims of religion have no reference to evolution. The soul of a Michael Angelo is of no superior value to the soul of a naked savage. The aim of freedom is advance in civilization, and the whole scale of its values lies between the life of a savage and the life of a Michael Angelo: or, if political freedom be considered, between the institutions of Dahomey and those of Great Britain. Its sole aim in the future is to increase that difference. None of these aims has any interest for religion. For that, all interest centres in the individual soul; and the standard of value is transcendental.

The second answer is that which was given by the Greeks. The proper guide of human conduct, they said, is wisdom; and by wisdom they meant knowledge, or a systematic acquaintance with all the facts of past experience. This might serve very well for a life whose conditions were stationary, and where the future contained no new elements beyond what were to be found in the past. But it is of only limited use in conditions which are marked by the continual appearance of new features, which are always unexpected, and which it is not given to human reason to foresee. A rule which is based exclusively on the past is fatal to adaptation, and it defeats, instead of promoting, the ends of freedom.

None of these objections apply to the conscience. That has no end of its own; or none, at any rate, with which we are acquainted. The essential character of its commands is that they must be obeyed without regard to consequences. The special function of the conscience is to support particular classes of impulses. It is not an impulse itself, but an arbiter between rival impulses when they conflict. And the weight of its authority is always thrown on the side of the weak, and against the strong. It supports the more recently evolved impulses of self-abnegation, which are useful to societies, against the more primitive and more powerful impulses of self-assertion; and, in this way, its influence is always in the direction of advance. Its effects, therefore, are always in accordance with the aim of freedom; that is to say, the elevation of human beings, in this life, to still higher levels beyond the stage of barbarism.

This explanation, so far as it goes, has no trace of mythology, or even of metaphysics. It implies nothing as to the origin, or the real nature, of the conscience, but concerns itself with the more fruitful question of what it does, or what are its natural functions. It attributes no gift of prescience. In fact, by making it indifferent to consequences, it implicitly denies that. The function of conscience being to strengthen the newer and more elevated types of impulse in every character, it follows that it should vary in accordance with the special needs of each individual character. And this we see it does. Men who are on a low level of ethical experience are hardly aware of its existence. Its highest point of development was perhaps in the inner voice of Socrates, in whom it took a form with which few of us are personally familiar. Its most widely diffused manifestation is in what we call conscientiousness; the quality which distinguishes a good workman from a bad one. The conscientious workman is he in whom the claims of his work prevail over his own dread of exertion. In its variety and still more in its capacity for development, the conscience resembles all the higher products of evolution. Its action is in exact harmony with the aims of freedom.

We shall find in the course of this inquiry that morality itself has its stages, which correspond with the succeeding stages in human development. Each individual has his separate conscience, which is adapted to his own personal character and needs. From the sum of the separate consciences of its citizens each nation derives a national morality, adapted to the prosecution of the national ideal. And, finally, all separate codes of morality are merged in a single system which has for its aim the elevation of the human race as a whole. Obedience to the moral law, in all stages of development, may properly be designated as wisdom. But at no stage can men afford to neglect the claims either of religion or of science. The progress of humanity must be harmonious and comprehensive. Wisdom by itself is of little avail, unless it is accompanied by both religious faith and scientific knowledge.

Political Freedom

We may proceed to the definition of political freedom. Man is a gregarious animal; that is to say, he combines with his fellows for the prosecution of a common end. The compromise which constitutes freedom is here raised to a higher level. The conflict of impulses within the individual is succeeded by the conflict of individuals within the community. Their activities clash, and each man's action curtails or controls the activities of his neighbours. In questions of external goods, such as property, this is obvious. Two men may be impelled to strive for the same piece of land, but both cannot enjoy the whole of it at the same time. The two ideas of effort and conflict are so intimately associated that the same word is used for both. In material interests, to strive implies strife.

Beyond the conflict for material goods, and on a higher ethical level than that, is the conflict between opinions, or beliefs. Its superior importance is reflected in the greater heat and bitterness with which it is waged; both between parties within a state, and between competing nations. Advocates of liberty at all price have urged that it is not a proper field for the intervention of government. But public opinion would itself be unhealthy if it supported government in tolerating the public utterance, by speech or in writing, of blasphemy, obscenity, or treason. The argument that any interference of that kind might bring about the destruction of new and valuable varieties of opinion deserves particular notice, as it tells against the case it is meant to support, and indicates its special dangers. A gardener who was advised to let weeds alone for fear he might extirpate new and valuable varieties of plants, would know that what would follow would be the destruction of all except the rankest varieties of weeds. What men want for their own use they must protect and mature by their own care. It is the same in the field of thought. In conditions of perfect liberty it is debased opinions that gain the upper hand, and the more elevated that go under. The law is indeed universal. No good habits of any kind, in any field of thought or action, can be acquired or maintained except by the painful and vigilant repression of bad habits.

Without a paramount end, which is common to all, or to a decisive majority, no collection of individuals can be called a community: there will be no co-ordination of interests and no freedom. Even so simple an event as a conflict between the savage inhabitants of adjoining tracts of country introduces a common end of action on each side. Each contends for its own existence and for the victory through which that is secured. To that extent the interest of every individual will be identical with that of every other in the same group; and common action will demand obedience, or the sacrifice of personal inclinations, to the authority of a chieftain. Individual liberty will give way to collective freedom. The idea of a social compact, when understood literally, is of course untrue; but, as a parable, it gives a serviceable notion of what actually took place. The whole process has been unconscious, but what it really amounted to was that individuals sacrificed to the state so much of their liberty as was necessary for the preservation of what they retained. The sacrifice was not voluntary but of necessity.

The collective existence of the community is the common end of all communities, in all stages of civilization; but in none is it the final or ultimate end. Existence is never worth having on its own account, but only for the use which is made of it. Communities, even in the earliest stages, differ in the objects for which they live. Abel was a shepherd, Cain an agriculturist. In the same way as life is the universal condition without which no man can realize his personal ends, so is collective existence the primary condition without which no community can realize theirs. And to prefer the life of the individual to the existence of the community is, by

ethical standards, to postpone a higher class of ends
to a lower. Moreover, it entails the sacrifice of all
that is valuable in the life of the individual himself.

*Political Justice universal condition of Political
Freedom*

Much learning and ingenuity have been devoted
to the elaboration of abstract political constitutions
which may serve to secure freedom against anarchy
on the one hand and despotism on the other. The
labour has not been wasted; it has indeed been
indispensable on the occurrence of crises, such as
the restoration of order after the French Revolution; the erection of a new state out of the revolted
colonies in America; and at least twice in the
course of English history; when the old political
conditions have been swept away and new ones
must be provided for. On such occasions it has
been the practice of the statesmen to whom the
task was committed to preface their practical proposals with a proclamation of what they believed to
be the essential and universal rights of humanity;
whose maintenance must be secured by all constitutions whatever, at all times and in all places.
There is, however, only one principle which is the
universal and necessary condition of political freedom; and that is, political justice, or justice in the
distribution of power and property.

Beneath the shifting mass of conflicting principles which must be combined for the prosecution of its common end by every civilized state, two are elementary and universal; quantity, or numbers; and quality, or personal merit. These always conflict, and the due recognition of both is political justice. In order that a state may be free, that is to say, maintain its further advance in the direction of its appointed end, it is necessary that it should secure, first, the freedom of every individual citizen, whatever his merits may be; and, secondly, the just reward for qualities which give to particular citizens a superior value. This is only the survival, under infinitely varied forms, of the primitive conflict between the undifferentiated mass of individuals and the aggression of the stronger.

The first and most important modification in the terms of this conflict arises from the impossibility of ascertaining an even approximately correct equation, applicable to single cases, between merit and reward. A partial solution to this difficulty has been discovered by making rewards, when they have once been gained, hereditary. Pascal observes with reference to this difficulty (*Pensées*, art. v, s. 3): 'The greatest of evils is civil war. That is certain to occur if people claim a reward for merit: for every one will assert merit for himself. The evils which may be apprehended from a fool who succeeds by right of birth are neither so great, nor so certain.' This expedient, though it may fail to correspond exactly with the theory of justice, has usually been found successful in maintaining, over considerable periods, the integrity of a state. A people who are accustomed to inequality of conditions will not be ready to question its justice in every particular instance; and they will be much more ready to acquiesce when the aristocracy has not crystallized in a closed caste. Every promotion from the ranks will be a fresh assertion of the principle; exceptional merit has always the hope of a sufficient, if not nicely calculated, reward; and a conventional inequality is not resented, so long as a real equality, which permits a man to rise from the lowest to the highest social level, is recognized; and still less when, through the wholesome rule of a primogeniture, men may descend from the highest to the lowest. The recognition of the hereditary principle with regard to material wealth will aim at the same result in a pure republic as is achieved under an aristocracy by hereditary rank, but not, perhaps, with the same success. It gives an undue preference to material ends, and to the faculties by which they are realized.

The function of law, and generally of state control, in that co-ordination of individuals for the prosecution of a common end which we call freedom, is to maintain internal peace by curbing the self-assertion of the strong, and preserving to the weak a reasonable scope for the exercise of their own activities. It follows, as a general principle, that the weaker party will appeal to the law, while the stronger will provide the champions of liberty. This principle, though it is often obscured, is not by any means obsolete. A despot has no need of law ; an aristocracy will uphold its claims in opposition to a king, and reduce him to the status of a limited monarchy. The owners of wealth, whether from commerce or from land, always demand fresh extensions of liberty, which they disguise under the sacred name of freedom. *Laissez faire,* freedom of trade, freedom of contract and of competition, are little more than demands for a return to the primitive state of chaos, when there was no freedom, and liberty was the monopoly of superior force. The lower, and more numerous classes, on the other hand, will ask for special laws for their protection, and, in the name of socialism, invest the state with an unlimited authority. They will not demand an extension of liberty until, through some social or political revolution, they have already gained the upper hand. These considerations apply, of course, only to a state where the conflict between weak and strong is still in progress. Where large classes have been altogether excluded from power, they will demand the complete destruction of political institutions, and leave neither law nor liberty.

The danger of civil war, or political disruption, against which we are warned by Pascal, will be dealt with later on, when we have determined what, for the purposes of freedom, we mean by a state or political community. For our present needs it is enough to say that the complete victory of either tendency will at once arrest evolution. The principle of personal equality, when it has realized itself in socialism, or in any form of pure democracy, can only be maintained by the elimination of originality, or individual eminence: the principle of reward for merit, when carried to its full length, annihilates the liberty of the masses, and ends in despotism. In both cases we arrive at a dead level, and in neither is there left any trace of the liberty, the maintenance and further development of which form the only justification for the control of law. Men were created strong and weak, wise and foolish, clever and dull; and civilization has added many new distinctions, such as rich and poor, noble and common. So long as distinctions survive, men will advance and prosper —but not longer. On the other hand, it is equally true and necessary that all men should have their due share of liberty, and be equal before the law.

Unless both these principles are recognized, there is no freedom and no progress. Rome retained her freedom and her power of expansion so long as political power was divided between the Senate and the people: when the people conquered she lost both.

Parties

Every question has two sides, and ordinary men are so constituted that they can no more see both at the same time, than they can, with their bodily vision, see both the sides of a closed door. A man's practical beliefs are not determined solely by his position in society, but rather by his whole philosophy of life, in which his ethical sentiments, however derived, and, still oftener, his religious beliefs, or want of belief, are the more potent ingredients. On all these points men will be divided, and it is well for healthy progress that they should be. In political questions, the main line of division will be drawn between the party of liberty and the party of law. With the exception of a few philosophers at one end of the scale, and, at the other, of men who are too indolent to take an interest in public affairs, the whole community will be split into two parties, each of which will be engaged in the promotion of one only of the two great conflicting aims whose clash gives birth to freedom, and maintains its life. Each will be blind to the claims of the other, or so nearly blind as to refuse them a just and equal hearing; and each will exaggerate to a degree, which to an impartial bystander must seem extravagant, the claims of his own. Nor is this arrangement without its use. If every citizen were an impartial judge there would be no conflict; and the whole community would lack the heat and emotional force on which its corporate life is dependent.

When a democracy clamours for more law, it is for party purposes, and as a weapon against political adversaries: not in the interest of the whole community, or as a protection against external dangers. And the same thing is true when the wealthy demand an extension of liberty. In this conflict the opposed principles are known in our own days as that of collectivism, and that of individualism. The former is the party of law, the latter of liberty; of a liberty, it is true, which Goethe describes as ' Willkür jeder für sich ', while he betrays his sympathies with the other side in his maxim ' Und das Gesetz kann nur uns Freiheit geben '. Both parties are equally necessary to the health of every political community, and their conflict will not be a source of weakness so long as they are ready to combine for the defence of the common ideal. It is only when they allow that to be eclipsed by their party ideals that they bring about a serious danger of disruption.

The cause of law always labours under one serious disadvantage. Law means restraint, or the sacrifice, in some measure, of what we desire, and its appeal lies to the higher instincts. Liberty, on the other hand, means the satisfaction of all desires, and needs no recommendation. When a hedonist philosophy of life is prevalent, the desires and the intellectual convictions point in the same direction, and the alliance will be well-nigh irresistible. For this, and for other reasons, the philosophy of pleasure will always be congenial to the party of wealth. The cause of freedom can only be rescued from defeat when the alliance between material prosperity and hedonist philosophy is opposed by the strongest possible demonstration on the part of the moral law.

The universal principle which is to be observed in the constitution of every free community must contain two features. In the first place it must combine, and not divide, the citizens; and, secondly, it must be common to all of them. The principle of the greatest happiness of the greatest number, as understood by those who profess it, fails in both respects. Material happiness is secured by material wealth, and the same item of material wealth, as we have already observed, can only be enjoyed by one man at a time. Two men cannot use the same shilling without dividing it. The pursuit of material happiness, therefore, divides and does not combine the citizens. The concrete example of the disputes between labour and capital brings this down to the level of obvious fact. Again, the term, 'the greatest number', necessarily implies the exclusion of some, and, possibly, of a considerable number, of the citizens; and, if any are excluded, there is no longer a community: those who are excluded are no longer citizens. Again, Bentham's formula entirely overlooks the claims of merit, and gives no principle for guiding the distribution of happiness. The coward and the hero stand on the same level. The proper formula for the constitution of a free state will be—the greatest possible activity of all, without exception. No happiness is of value unless it follows, as a reward, on activity.

Value of Freedom

This seems all that need be said at present about the general conditions of freedom. We will next endeavour to account for its supremacy among the moral values; a position in which its only rival is justice. But there can be no freedom without justice, and no security for justice except freedom; for the justice of a despot depends on his personal qualities, and will seldom survive him. The two are mutually interdependent; they have no separate interests, and it is impossible that they should in any way be brought into conflict. The values of both are equal, and rest on a common ground.

There is no necessary connexion between freedom and happiness. The stock instance of diffused happiness is the era of the Antonines, under a despotism; and it is certain that people have often been happy under a despot. The reign of Peisistratus affords another illustration. For the true explanation of the value of freedom we need not travel beyond its definition. Freedom is the necessary condition for the exercise of the greatest possible number and diversity of activities, first within each individual, and then within a political community; that is to say, in both, for the release of the greatest possible degree and variety of power; and, as the increase of power is the index of advance in civilization, it is that which gives freedom its pre-eminent value. Happiness, as in the era of the Antonines, and as there was some reason to fear it might be in our own time, is not inconsistent with decay. On the other hand, though freedom need not produce happiness, it always determines its value. The happiness of a free man is worth having: that of a slave is not. The Belgians prefer unhappiness with freedom to the prospect of happiness under a German governor; because, in the latter case,

VALUE OF FREEDOM 27

they would lose all prospect of national development.

All progress towards an end is conditioned by conflict; and the extent of the progress is proportionate to the intensity and variety of the activities which the conflict calls into play. The common end of an individual is his self-development, and his progress is dependent on the conflict of the various internal impulses which make up his whole character. A perfectly consistent character, from which all conflict had been eliminated, would be satisfied with the position it had already gained, and would feel no call for improvement. Such a man would soon be outstripped by others who were not equally well satisfied with themselves.

In the same way, the common end of a political society is its own development; and, for further development, or increase of strength, it is dependent on conflict of interests between individuals and parties among its own citizens. A perfectly homogeneous community, which had no internal dissensions, is only possible in a state of stagnation. In a free community the only point on which all need be united is the prosecution of the common end which unites them. To this, it is true, all other ends must be subordinate. The citizens must at all times, in peace as well as in war, be united against a common foe, but, without conflicting interests among themselves, there is no prospect of any increase in the force with which they can oppose him. England has to thank party for her growth, and the subordination of party to national ends for her safety.

In the same way as the growth of the individual depends on the conflict of internal impulses, and the growth of the community on the conflict of internal interests, so does the human race as a whole depend for its evolution on the conflict of national ends or ideals. Further than this we are unable to go. All the conflicts on which the evolution of the race is dependent are between opposed elements within itself. The only universal interests of humanity are, first, that the conflict should continue, and, secondly, that the evil principle, or principle of degeneration, should not gain a decisive advantage over the good principle, or principle of advance.

Thus we find, within the range of ethics, a hierarchy of ends, culminating with the supreme end of the evolution, or advance to a higher level, of the human race as a whole. This advance gives the ultimate standard of ethical value, and it rests, as a necessary base, on two subordinate classes of value, those, namely, of the evolution of the individual, and of the evolution of the body politic. All these three are mutually interdependent. It is impossible to realize any one of them in the absence of the other two; and the indispensable condition for advance in the cases both of the individual and of the body politic is freedom. There can be no free individuals in a state which is either anarchic or under a despotic government; there can be no free state when the individual citizens either have no respect for duty, or are at the mercy of their passions: and there can be no advance in the race as a whole, without advance both in the individuals and in the communities out of which the race is constituted. Freedom then, both moral and political, is the keystone of evolution, and the essential condition for the realization of the highest values.

The conflict of opposed ideals, which is the universal form in which evolution exhibits itself to our observation, introduces another link in the chain which connects the freedom of the individual with the development of the race. A nation loses its power to maintain its ideal as soon as it is conquered by a nation with an opposed ideal. It then drops out of the world-conflict, and becomes worthless for the purposes of evolution. National independence, then, is another essential condition for human progress. It is only in an independent state that men can be free in themselves or in their relations with their neighbours, and, on the other hand, it is only where men and institutions are free that national independence can be maintained for long. The necessity is reciprocal.

Ideals national—not universal

The use of the word nation in the last few paragraphs was unavoidable; but it was premature, and must now be justified. Our object was to show that the progress of humanity as a whole, which is the supreme ethical end, is conditioned by two subordinate stages of progress, first, that of the individual, and, secondly, that of the society; progress in both these stages being dependent on freedom. For practical purposes every one knows what is an individual, and the term needs no definition. What, for the purposes of practical politics, is to be understood by a political unit is not equally obvious. The question has given rise to conflicting interpretations, and the recognition of independent communities with separate claims, apart from the claims which are common to the whole of humanity, has been the subject of a controversy which up to the time of the Reformation was of paramount interest in the world of political thought; and which, even now, has not been finally disposed of.

Community of aim or ideal is not by itself sufficient to distinguish a political society. Where-ever two or more individuals are associated together there must be a common aim. We may leave out minor associations, such as those for the purposes of trade and commerce, of plunder, or of missionary enterprise, which have a common end, but have never been regarded as political units, and proceed to consider the case of municipal governments. These have been during long periods of history, and over large areas of the world's surface, political units; and the principals through whose conflicts the advance of civilization has been secured. But they are so no longer, and in the loss of that position we discover the distinctive feature which constitutes a political unit. That distinctive feature is sovereignty; or an internal authority, however vested, which enacts and enforces the law, but is not itself amenable to it. In its want of accountability, and its absolute authority, sovereignty, in an ideal state, holds a position which is closely analogous to that which is held by conscience in an ideal man. A sovereign community is a state, whether it be a village or an empire. But neither may the conscience be identified with the man nor the sovereign with the community. In both they are only the governing principles. Their complete independence of control might seem to entitle both the conscience and sovereign power to the attribution of perfect liberty. But it would only be by a metaphor. Neither liberty nor freedom can be properly predicated except of whole individuals or communities. They presume internal conflict: in the first, the conflict of impulses; in the second, of private interests.

Loss of independence necessarily involves loss of sovereignty. The internal authority is no longer absolute, but under the control of an external power. The community in which it formerly resided is no longer a political unit; nor can it enjoy political freedom. The small Greek city-states were independent political units, and their continual conflicts among themselves were attended by a rapid growth in civilization in all its branches, such as has never been equalled either before or since. When they became subject to the Macedonian Empire the growth was at once arrested, and soon ceased altogether. The people of Athens remained, but not the sovereignty. In order that a people may be sovereign it must be organized under fixed rules, and must declare and execute its will with recognized formalities. It is then distinguished from a mob. An ἐκκλησία is no longer a σύνοδος.

At the commencement of our era the whole of western civilization was under the undivided sovereignty of Imperial Rome. There was no longer any conflict of states or state ideals. The growth of civilization was at once arrested; nor was it resumed till eight centuries later, when the seeds were sown of a new conflict. The ideals of both the Empire and the Papacy were universal: one was centred in this world; the other in the world to come, and the dispute was ended by the emergence of a number of national states, each with its independent national ideal; and a number of independent forms of the same religion, which nearly, though not exactly, corresponded with the number of states. The system of competing national ideals, under which we now live, has been the parent of our modern civilization.

It would be a mistake to suppose that the dispute between religion and civil government has been completely disposed of, or that it could be disposed of by a comprehensive toleration of all kinds of religious beliefs; and, as the point is of vital consequence in its bearings on freedom, I propose to take this opportunity of noticing it. Complete autonomy, whether of religion or of the conscience, is, and always must be, in theory at least, incompatible with civil sovereignty. Of this, the following case will serve at once as illustration and proof.

A considerable number of individual citizens may base a claim to be exempted from service in the army, on the plea that their religion, or their conscience, or perhaps both, forbid them to bear arms, or to take life. To this plea there is one sufficient answer: the whole duty of a nation, as represented by its government, is to preserve its own existence for the maintenance of its national ideal. It may be necessary to place every able-bodied citizen in the field; and of this necessity the sovereign government is, and, of its essence, always must be, the sole judge. To admit the validity of any such plea would be to recognize the claims of an external and superior authority, and the civil power would thereby abdicate its sovereignty. From these considerations emerges a very important maxim: whenever a universal end comes into conflict with a national end the former must give way. The universal end itself can only be realized by the observance of this rule: for the advance of civilization will not survive the destruction of national ideals; and a national ideal ceases to exist when the nation ceases to be independent.

On the other hand, though national sovereignty must repel all dictation from universal ideals, it must not on that account be blind to their influence. If it subjects them to unnecessary contradiction or outrage, it will soon forfeit its own authority. Fortunately, the principle in this case, though it claims to be universal, is not so in fact. If a religion is to be judged by its collective authority, and not identified with the opinions which are held by some of its sects, it is certain that Christianity has never condemned the profession of a soldier, but has, over and over again, enjoined war in a just cause. From the beginning, Christians served in the army; at first few, and, at the time of the conversion of the Empire, in very large numbers. Soldiers contributed more than their fair proportion to the roll of Christian saints and martyrs. The only authoritative pronouncement against enlistment was when the Council at Nicaea forbade Christians to serve under the pagan Licinius against the Christian Constantine (Harnack, *Mission und Ausbreitung*, 395). This difficulty is especially likely to arise under a government which respects all religious opinions impartially. The greater the number and the variety of opinions, the stronger is the likelihood of a collision between the government and one or more of them.

Though this has been the ruling of the universal Church, and of its principal branches up to the present day, there has, of course, been much dissent. Sects like the Quakers, and many before them, have disputed it; but some have been explicitly condemned, and nearly all have died out, not from persecution, but from spontaneous exhaustion, and loss of adherents. They have nearly always forgotten that their doctrine forms part of a system, and has no independent validity. The command, turn the other cheek, is no more binding than the command, sell all thou hast and give to the poor. If a man will not fight, neither should he trade, or, indeed, marry. These are all precepts in a system of complete renunciation of worldly interests; and one of them by itself has no justification without the rest. It is clear that the adoption of the whole system, or, indeed, of any of its precepts, would bring about the complete destruction, not only of society, but of the whole human race. Without marriage or trade, or the right of self-defence, the present order of things must come to an end. A nation has no more right to take the risk of destruction than a man has to commit suicide. To maintain life, and make the best of it, is a duty which is common to both. If a man would withdraw from the conflict, he must become a monk.

Another instance, this time of conscience and not religion, is that of conscientious objections to vaccination. This, though of vastly inferior practical importance, is of equal value as a question of principle. Its insignificance may or may not justify its recognition; but mere neglect involves no abdication of its supreme authority on the part of the state. If thereby the health and lives of large numbers of citizens, whose conscience was differently constituted, were seriously imperilled, the recognition would no doubt be withdrawn.

When public safety on the one side, and private religion or conscience on the other are in opposition, there can be neither submission nor compromise. The first is the duty of the state, the second, of the individual, and, for both, duty is supreme. The man who, for bribe or menace, disobeys his private conscience, and the government which, for any reason, yields to its claims when they are adverse, are both traitors—the man against himself, the government against the country of whose welfare it is the guardian. The only escape for the individual is martyrdom, and to the nation itself its martyrs are no disgrace; while they, by universal consent, have exhibited in themselves the highest form of virtue, and are, therefore, deserving of the highest form of happiness as their reward; but that reward they ought to look for elsewhere; and, when they are sincere, they do.

No religion, however advanced, has condemned war unconditionally. The church which proclaimed the truce of God, at the same time preached the Crusades. But in all its modern forms it has demanded a valid motive, and it has attempted, with much success, to mitigate its ferocity, discharging, in this way, some of the functions of an international tribunal. The absence of religion from a national ideal is an unmixed evil. If common to both sides, it brings all the combatants nearer

38 IDEALS NATIONAL—NOT UNIVERSAL

to the level of brutes; if peculiar to one, that side only. And when they differ on this point the victory of one will promote, of the other, throw back, the cause of civilization. But it must operate from within, and conform itself to the other features of the national ideal. It must be structural, and not parasitic.

A third universal end of freedom, besides the realization of the aims of religion, or of the individual conscience, has been found in the realization of the aims of morality. This however is irreconcilable with national freedom, for the same reason which applies in the case of religion. One nation differs from another as greatly in its moral ideals as it does in its religious, and to enforce uniformity would be to destroy the mechanism by which evolution is now effecting its ends. The destruction of a nation's moral ideal would be the same thing as the destruction of its freedom; and this, besides being highly undesirable, is not within the range of practical politics. This conclusion however, though true in itself, is not in conflict with a wider conception, which has not yet been distinctly formulated, though its hold over the more advanced peoples is daily increasing in strength. That is the conception of a community of nations, which, having for its connecting principle the advancement of the human race as a whole, should stand in the same relation to the freedom of nations as that does to the freedom of the individual. The legislation of a community of that kind would be guided by the aims of a universal morality. On this subject we hope to add a few words later on.

As an universal ideal, common to the whole of humanity, neither religion nor morality is at all likely to supplant the various national ideals whose conflict is the primary condition of human development. The mischief they do is indirect, and consists in running counter to the spirit of patriotism, and deadening its influence. They find their expression in discordant and irrelevant councils; and the leaders of the people will cry aloud, like Ajax, for deliverance from the cloud which blinds and paralyses their soldiers.

Distinctions of Nationality.

All types of institution change and become obsolete. The principle of nationality as the bond which holds together a political unit, and opposes it to other units, can expect no exemption. It has only recently emerged into full recognition, and may be destined to further extension and development, but it is not likely to escape supersession, sooner or later, by some wider and more comprehensive principle. What that will be it is useless to speculate. Sufficient for our purpose are the facts of to-day. The principle of nationality has been objected to as elusive, and not susceptible of exact definition. Whether this be true or not, it lives, and works, and must be reckoned with, and, as far as possible, understood. We may proceed to consider very shortly what are its qualifications for the position which it occupies in our own days. The more abstract question of a general principle of growth, which has already substituted the nation for the city state, and may, problematically, substitute great ethical or religious beliefs in the place of the nation, is altogether beyond our scope.

Nationality is originally based upon race, or community of blood. When pushed back into the region of mythical origins, it implies that all the members of the community are descended from a common ancestor. This fiction, though of course not an historical fact, has an historical value, in calling attention to, and furnishing a plausible explanation of what is an undoubted fact. The members of a nation are distinguished by a common resemblance which is roughly comparable to that resemblance between members of the same family which we call family likeness. In neither case is the distinction infallible, but in a great majority of instances it is unmistakable. A difference in nationality will be suspected, where it exists, after a few minutes conversation with a stranger. It is not worth our while to inquire how this distinction of national type comes into existence. But a few words ought to be said about one at least of the causes by which it is protected, and the uses which ensue from it.

Primitive history was not far wrong in dating the origin of nationality from the tower of Babel. Distinctions of language lie at the root of all historical developments, and the restoration of a universal form of speech might, not improbably, arrest or reverse the process. Unless peoples had been united among themselves, and segregated from others, by this powerful barrier, the units of family and tribe would never have been merged in the larger unit of nationality. Physical barriers by themselves are an insufficient protection. Two of the strongest natural fortresses in the world are Great Britain, with her sea, and India with her gigantic mountain ranges, but both have been overcome. In India, where the process has been many times repeated, the results are too complex to be dealt with here. In England, the conquerors and the conquered have been amalgamated in a new nationality by a new language, which preserves, and in its literature gives expression to, the most serviceable elements in the respective characters of each of the united peoples. The ideal to which Shakespeare gave a permanent literary form has supplied the foundations to the national character in all lands beyond the seas in which the English language is spoken. The long eclipse of nationality during the contest between Pope and Emperor was only achieved by the retention of Latin as the sole literary medium. Dante was the necessary precursor to the growth and unification of the Italian nation.

Differences of language, by making the people of different nations mutually unintelligible, have put a bar to that intimate conversation which is the indispensable preliminary to a mutual sympathy and respect; and, when added to differences in appearance and manner, not only act as an additional obstacle to intercourse, but give rise to a mutual antipathy and antagonism which men always feel towards what they neither understand nor trust. Before improved means of communication had weakened the force of geographical barriers, these feelings often led to the prohibition of intermarriage, or of eating together at the same table; expressions of disgust, which, though not unknown among classes within the same nation, are not then reinforced by barriers of race and language. Other distinguishing characteristics are national gods, national forms of worship, and customs and traditions, all culminating in a complex national ideal; and the total mass is amply sufficient for the differ-

DISTINCTIONS OF NATIONALITY 43

entiation of opposed units in the conflict on which all advance in civilization is dependent. Of the survival of international hatred in our own days we have had sufficient proof, though it may be stronger in some nations than in others.

It is not to be supposed that these distinctions, and the feelings they engender, are good in themselves, or deserving of approbation. On the contrary they are in direct contradiction to peace, charity, and happiness; which, in the judgement of the great majority of mankind, are the goods which are most to be desired. But they are as essential to further evolution as self-sacrifice is; and advance in civilization is the highest ethical good, which conditions advance in all the goods which we really value. We must remember that the effects of international hatred are not confined to the period of war, but only reach their full strength in the period which immediately follows it. The relations between the conquerors and the conquered will then be embittered by contempt on the one side and humiliation and disappointment on the other, and, on both, by an active desire for revenge for recent injuries. In the meantime, all the distinctions of language and appearance will remain, and the increased bitterness will spend itself exclusively on the weaker or conquered people. They need expect neither mercy, nor consideration.

PRACTICAL APPLICATIONS

WITH SPECIAL REFERENCE
TO UNIVERSAL MILITARY SERVICE

Εἷς οἰωνὸς ἄριστος ἀμύνεσθαι περὶ πάτρης

PRACTICAL APPLICATIONS

RELATION BETWEEN FREEDOM AND UNIVERSAL MILITARY SERVICE

Preliminary

THE peculiar duty, then, of every nation is the maintenance, development, and propagation of its own ideal; and freedom is the sole universal condition under which this duty can be accomplished. Slavery, in one form or another, is the penalty for neglect, and that extinguishes, at the same time, both the duty and the means of accomplishing it. Before proceeding further we must notice and explain what is a very common fallacy. Men often say that they go to war with full confidence in the justice of their cause. If by this they mean that they are ready to run all risks rather than betray the sacred cause of justice, this is a very noble and inspiring sentiment; it is the spirit of martyrdom, than which nothing can be more valuable. But if they mean that they trust to the justice of their cause for success, nothing could be more delusive, or fraught with more manifold dangers. In the first place, they have only their own opinion to go on as to the justice of their cause. In the second, in conditions of evolution, injustice has almost as good a prospect of success as justice. History shows us that sometimes one prevails, at others, the other. To trust to the merits of your cause without taking the necessary means to maintain it, is to betray it, as surely as if you declined to expose yourself to any risks whatever. And the principal of those means is self-sacrifice. What a nation must rely on is not the goodness of its cause, but its own right arm, and the manliness of its citizens: and the better the cause, the more ignominious is its betrayal.

If we leave out of consideration the personal qualities and beliefs of the individual citizens, which are the subject of general ethics, the survival of a national ideal is dependent on the strength of the national government by which it is represented. And this question must be considered under two aspects, which are so closely connected and interdependent that neither can be dealt with separately. The first is the relations of the government with other nations; the second, its relations with its own citizens. Mistakes in one case lead to the loss of independence; in the other, to internal disruption; and in both to the destruction of the national ideal. Success, in its foreign relations depends on the measures which are taken by the government for utilizing to the best effect all the resources which are at its disposal; in its internal relations, on its justice, and on nothing else. We have already explained what we mean by justice. A nation is free so long as its institutions are just, and no longer.

For the measures which it should adopt in the marshalling of its resources, a nation must be guided by the nature of its resources which it has at its disposal; and that again is largely determined by the direction in which its activities have been habitually exercised. Whatever that may be, there is only one practical end for all. The production of the greatest possible amount of strength or power, in subordination to their diverse ideals, is the common immediate end of all nations, as it is of every separate individual, and of the whole human race when regarded under the aspect of evolution. For the maintenance of its freedom and independence, a nation requires the utmost attainable degree of power. Not an ounce can be spared. It is futile to talk of degrees of power, or to calculate how much is required in order to meet all known contingencies. The wisest statesman has nothing but probability to guide him, and, the wider his range of vision, the greater will be his distrust of what lies beyond it. His aim will be to provide against all dangers, whether foreseen or unforeseen; and for that purpose he requires the maximum of activities of all kinds, co-ordinated for the single end of national independence.

Commercial and Military Ideals

Material power, and it is that with which we are at present concerned, takes two forms, and is represented either by material wealth, or by material or brute force; and these may be regarded in the light of opposed ideals. All other forms of power, such as religion, or science, or moral qualities, may be used in support of both of these, and are not peculiar to either, though their characters will be profoundly modified by reaction to the cause in which they are employed. The morality of a merchant is not the same as the morality of a soldier. When regarded as separate ideals, the former may be denoted as commercial, and the temper which it generates, as commercialism; the other as military, and its appropriate temper, as militarism. The combination of the two, in a proper proportion, produces the greatest attainable volume of material power. Either of them, by itself, or in undue predominance over the other, leads to weakness and degeneration. A short account of the main features of each kind of temper

COMMERCIAL AND MILITARY IDEALS 51

will assist us in stating the main practical problems with which the maintenance of freedom is confronted. Purely spiritual forces, like that of the Papacy, when it acquired its political supremacy in Europe without the help of a single soldier, lie outside of the province of political freedom.

The Military Spirit

The distinguishing virtues of militarism are those which are called forth by the necessities of an army in the field. Every soldier knows that his own safety, and that of his comrades, is dependent on his immediate and unquestioning obedience to orders. He learns to sacrifice both his judgement and his will, and, on occasion, his life. He thus acquires a temper which though not identical with patriotism—for he may be a mercenary—is at least akin to it, and prepares him for its reception. Again, a life in the field is the best remedy for softness and indolence, and prepares a man to accept privations and fatigue, in their most deterrent forms, without complaint. While he is on service, every soldier must be, in the best sense of the word, an ascetic. Courage, endurance, and submission to authority, with their cognate virtues, may be summed up in English as manliness; which, in *virtus*, its Latin equivalent, denoted the sum of all qualities that deserve respect. Areté, the Greek equivalent for virtue, and Arés, the name of the War god, are variations of the same word. In our own religion the military spirit retains nearly the same favour. In its collective form it describes itself as the Church Militant; its individual members are Christian soldiers. The New Testament abounds with similar metaphors. 'Fight the good fight'; 'Put on the whole armour of God'; and so forth.—On the other hand, its sympathies are not with commerce. Trade with the Spirit was the sin of Simon Magus. Thomas à Kempis bids us,[1] 'Give up all things, abandon all you desire, and you will find rest. This is the epitome of religious perfection.' The aim of the monk was rest; but the spirit was the same as that of the soldier, when he gives up all things, and leaves all that he loves, at the call of his country.

The chief virtue of militarism, before which all the others recede into the background, is that it strongly inculcates the spirit of cohesion. Every soldier knows that, in order to gain the end of the enterprise on which he is engaged, he must regard himself, not as an isolated individual, but as an integral part of the whole force. This solidarity of purpose is the highest of political virtues, and in its absence no political community can retain either

[1] *De Imitatione Christi*, iii. 52.

its internal freedom, or its national independence. *Esprit de corps* is a soldier's virtue and we fetch our name for it from France. It is the same thing as patriotism, but in a more restricted province.

Against the virtues of militarism must be reckoned its vices. The same circumstances which produce indifference to suffering in ourselves destroy pity and compassion for the sufferings of others, and, unless his temper is raised by impulses derived from another source, which is not military, a man is brought to a level below that of wolves and tigers. For cruelty is almost peculiar to him, and, while they are merely indifferent to the sight of pain, he will take pleasure in it, and seek it for its own sake. Hatred, no doubt, adds to the fury of a soldier's onset, and it adds at the same time to the pleasure which he takes in the torture of an enemy who is at his mercy. That this is not merely an abstract probability is shown by examples other than that of the Red Indians, and in races whose culture is far higher than theirs. It is needless to speak of the other vices, such as lust, envy, and arrogance, which, though they are common to all conditions of life, find in the military spirit their favourite soil. A race of soldiers, unless the bestial side of its character has been tempered by a large infusion of the instincts of peace, will be incapable of the deference to the wishes and the interests of others which is essential to freedom ; and even its virtues will predispose it to the acceptance of servitude. It will not tolerate in others a blessing of which it knows itself to be incapable.

The military spirit, then, tells in the direction of control or law, and, as no one has ever identified law with freedom, or is likely to, it is not necessary to attempt a fuller description. All that we require is a general indication of its tendencies. With liberty the case is different. Liberty tells in the same direction as our desires, and is indeed nothing but the condition for their immediate gratification. It is therefore natural that men who have not paid much attention to the problems of life should, without inquiry, have identified it with freedom ; a thing which is admitted on all hands to be of the highest value, and in which liberty does, in fact, constitute the most prominent half. The tendency of commerce is in the direction of liberty, and in the following section of our subject the treatment must be much fuller.

The Commercial Spirit

Of all the conditions under which commerce can be successfully prosecuted the most essential is peace. The saying 'We go to war that we may be at peace' breathes the spirit of commerce, and would be out of place in the mouth of a soldier. And it is not true. Peace may be had without war, and without honour, by submission. When men go to war it is for freedom, and rather than lose that they would forego peace, and live in perpetual warfare. In this choice they are quite reasonable. Peace without freedom is valueless. It brings with it none of the blessings of peace—not even indolence and luxury, to say nothing of the higher values.

The spirit which is bred in a camp, and that which is bred by peaceful intercourse, differ in almost every particular, and are mutually antipathetic. The soldier and the tradesman are apt to regard one another with the unfriendly feelings which always animate the followers of opposed ideals; and an estrangement is set up between them which, though much less in degree, resembles both in origin and in nature the mutual hostility of separate nations. Neither side is likely to do justice to the good qualities of the other. In England the martial spirit was for long represented by the landed aristocracy. It was only with the immense development of manufactures, a movement which was largely assisted by the aristocracy themselves, through measures inspired by a purely commercial spirit, that the military spirit began to lose the precedence.

The leading virtue of commerce is charity. It is

to its interest to live in peace with all men, and not to be betrayed by anger and ill-feeling into conduct which may alienate customers. The deference, which is enjoined by interest, is closely allied to a genuine humility, which is slow to take offence, or to avenge injuries. To a merchant or a banker the solvency of his customers is of almost equal consequence with his own, and all growth in their prosperity will cause in him an almost equal satisfaction. Their interests (at least for a long way) are identical; in impoverishing them he impoverishes himself; and though, of course, he must himself take the precedence, he loves them (nearly) as well as he loves himself. Thus it comes that the Quakers, and similar sects, in whom one aspect of Christianity is strongly developed at the expense of its opposite, are distinguished for success in commerce. That the churches show less sympathy with them than might have been expected is perhaps due to the fact that however much they may love their neighbour they still put themselves in the first place, and not on an equality with him. The word love is indeed misplaced, and among men of commerce is seldom used except with reference to the loves of the market-place. The words by which they denote their own feelings, so far as they partake of altruism, are benevolence, charity, philanthropy, kindness, human sympathy, and the rest. And quite rightly. No two characters are more unlike than the lover and the benefactor. One lays down his life for his friend: the other pays for his education.

Allied with charity are the compassion for the sufferings of others, which finds expression in the erection and endowment of public hospitals; and the regard for their intellectual welfare, to which we owe a great number of our colleges and schools. The same spirit, acting in the sphere of religion, equips and maintains expensive missionary enterprises, which, again, promote the expansion of commerce. One of the most characteristic exhibitions of this spirit was the enfranchisement of our slaves, and the measures we have since taken for the suppression of slavery elsewhere, and for improving the character and the prospects of the free negro. It is seen at its best in the relations of a mother state with its colonies, or with countries which it acquires rather by annexation than by conquest. A federal empire, in which all the component states are free, is beyond the dreams of the military spirit.

With the other blessings of peace we are so familiar that it would be waste of time to recount them. Order, tranquillity, popular contentment, plenty, prosperity, advance in arts and science, literature, refinement, splendour; these are the fruits of commerce, and of peaceful liberty, so long as it remains uncorrupted. It may be called the source of all earthly blessings, with the exception of the spirit which defends them. With the corruptions of liberty we are equally familiar, but their correction runs counter to our desires, and to them we are often blind.

Special Dangers of Commercialism to Personal Character

Commerce, peace, and liberty, on the one hand, are opposed to militarism, war, and law and self-control, on the other, as two organic wholes. It is impossible to have either liberty or law without the appropriate spirit which gives life to each: and it is impossible to have freedom and national independence without both. Defects in liberty are defects in the spirit which gives it life and in the institutions in which it expresses itself; and, whether in the individual or in the state, they always, and must, of necessity, take the form of hostility to law. With the individual, in his relations with his inner nature, it is a refusal to submit to the voice of conscience and the general control of the laws of morality: in his public relations it is impatience with the laws of his country and the control of its government that

DANGERS OF COMMERCIALISM

endanger the cause of freedom. The following pages will be taken up with as brief an account as is consistent with our purpose of some of the concrete forms in which this hostility exhibits itself. Our description, it is hoped, will leave no doubt that the close connexion which we have asserted to exist between moral or personal, and political or national freedom, is more than a mere abstract hypothesis: that it is, indeed, a vital fact. Defects in both have a common origin, identical results, and common remedies; and to ignore the connexion is to imperil, and eventually to lose, all that makes life worth having.—Germany, in the present crisis, suffers from excess of law ; England, from excess of liberty. In neither are the conditions of freedom properly fulfilled.

The first effect of successful commerce is to emancipate the desires by removing all obstacles to their immediate gratification. This indeed, with most men, is the designed result or purpose of commerce; and, whether the desires be low or elevated in themselves, it is liberty, and nothing else. This immense access of liberty breeds a dislike and contempt for the moral law. The first of the virtues enjoined by the moral law is self-sacrifice: commerce supplies every facility for self-indulgence; and, to the commercial spirit, every form of asceticism or self-denial is ludicrous. The man who practises it, in however small a matter, is judged a fool. Luxury may be defined as impatience with small inconveniences, the dread of a rose leaf in a bed of feathers. It incapacitates men for the endurance of their own pain, and even for the most necessary infliction of pain on criminals and enemies. The conscience on the other hand teaches that neither pleasure nor pain, whether our own or in others, counts for anything in comparison with the fulfilment of its own commands. And there is far worse beyond. These are the roots of evil; not the flowers.

Near akin to luxury is indolence. The two are joined together in common speech; they are always found together; and they proceed from the same source; that is impatience with the control of the moral law. Rest, or what hedonist philosophy is pleased to call harmony, is no doubt pleasant, but we live by conflict, and the plain facts of life, in agreement with the moral law, enjoin labour, and leave no alternative but voluntary labour or slavery. If a man will not work for himself he will surely work for another; and in either case he will live by the sweat of his brow. The doom is inexorable, and when, seduced by plenty, he declines to work for his own cause, a degeneracy of character sets in, which makes him an easy prey to a less degenerate enemy. The desire for enjoyment combined with a dislike for work produces dishonesty, and his character parts with another element of strength in its loss of truthfulness. A man who is self-indulgent, slothful, and untrustworthy is of no use either to himself or to others; and this is the certain fate of the individual who, preferring moral liberty to moral freedom, refuses to submit to the control of his conscience.

Another source of danger to freedom in a commercial state, though it has no direct connexion with the moral law, has a very material effect on the national character, and must not be left unnoticed. Commerce is, in existing conditions, mainly dependent on ships, and must, for its own protection, provide itself with a powerful navy. This introduces considerations which are important everywhere, but of especial importance in a country like our own, which is inaccessible by land. A people who are prejudiced by commerce against militarism, and who are adverse to hardship, will welcome a protection which costs them nothing in personal danger; and it is certain that they will greatly overrate its value. They forget that safety demands that they shall put forth all the strength of which they are capable; that manliness counts for more than money; and that even if they sacrifice the whole of their money (which is most unlikely) they will still make use of less than half their strength;

and, finally, they overlook the lesson, enforced on them by history, that supremacy in naval power has often changed hands. In the threefold root of freedom—moral freedom, political freedom, and national independence—these dangers affect the last. But the danger to character is not less real. The military virtues are atrophied for want of exercise; debased forms of amusement take the place of drill; and to the vices of self-indulgence, indolence, and dishonesty, will be added insubordination, and a spirit so nearly resembling cowardice as not easily to be distinguished from it. This is not mere declamation. It will cost no long journey to observe the process of degeneration in full course in every grade of society.

Much more might be said about the degeneration of personal character which is brought about by the emancipation of liberty from law; but this must suffice. Our object, as we have already indicated, is not to give an exhaustive account of a subject which really embraces all the relations of human life, but merely to dispel the mischievous confusion of thought which identifies liberty with freedom, and puts the former in the place of the latter as the supreme end of all our efforts. This error is of exactly the same class as the view which identifies justice with equality, and takes no account of inequalities of personal merit. The next section will deal with the relations of liberty to political freedom, that is to say, to the community as represented by its government.

Dangers to Freedom in National Government

The special function of government is, we may repeat, the abolition of anarchy, that is to say, the protection of the weak against the strong; and, in a free state, it will discharge this function in such a way as to secure to every individual as much liberty as is consistent with the liberty of all the others. In the distribution of liberty it must be guided by justice. That is to say, it must pay equal attention to the conflicting claims of numbers and of merit. So long as it continues to represent the community it is sovereign, and must be obeyed. Its strength is the strength of the nation, and all action that tends to weaken that is treason to the national interests. It is impossible that a government should be too strong. It becomes oppressive, not through its strength, but only when it curtails unnecessarily the liberties of the whole, or of any particular section, of the community. A tyranny may be weak, but it is always oppressive, because it allows no legal liberty to any of its subjects. A socialist state will be oppressive, because it denies its due share of liberty to eminence in merit; and a pure aristocracy or plutocracy, because it refuses to recognize the liberties of the undistinguished multitude.

The institutions of a free state may be considered under two heads: first, the substantive law; and secondly, the government, including both the executive and the legislature. No distinction was made in the preceding paragraph between these various forms of control.

Of the substantive law little need be said except that it must be clear and certain. If it fails on either of these points it becomes expensive in its interpretation, or irregular in its execution. The poor, for whose protection law is especially designed, are debarred from using it, and it becomes an additional weapon in the hands of the wealthy. Moreover, this evil, like most other evils, grows. The interpretation of the law gives rise to a separate profession of lawyers, whose direct interest it is to increase both its obscurity and the uncertainty of its operation. One of the first interests of freedom is that the law should be popular, and that the courts should be easily accessible and speedy and certain in their processes.

Next after decay of character, the worst danger to freedom in a commercial state arises in the substitution of material ends, or, in a word, of money, in the place of the national ideal. Strictly speaking, money can never be a collective end, as a national end must be, if it is to command the common allegiance of all the citizens. However much a man may desire that his country should be wealthy, he never desires that it should be wealthy at his own expense. He toils for his own riches; and the enrichment of his nation, if he thinks of it at all, is a secondary consideration. The pursuit of money calls for no sacrifice of the self to the community, and, as an ideal, it is essentially disruptive.

The commanding attraction of money lies in its universality as a medium of exchange. It spares men all the risk and responsibility of specialization in their aims. At one time a man's heart may be set on the pleasures of the senses, at another on political power, or on social distinction; and his taste in pleasures may vary from time to time between the highest and the lowest forms of self-indulgence. Any section of his life which he devotes to one of these aims is largely, or wholly, thrown away when his tastes change and he turns to the pursuit of another. But this objection does not apply in the case of money. If he has that, all kinds of material gratification are potentially within his reach, and he can alter the direction of his expenditure whenever it suits him to do so. So long as he has money he feels safe, whatever may happen. This not only recommends the pursuit of money, but at the same time, by diverting his attention, obscures the attraction of all other ends, even when they are material. With the pursuit of ideal or spiritual ends it is, of course, quite incompatible. It tends to absorb, and so far as it prevails, does in fact absorb, a man's whole being. And the higher and more abstract ends are the first to disappear. A man may be a good tradesman, and at the same time a good father and husband, but seldom a good citizen.

The extreme development of the abstract theory of commercial liberty was reached in the writings of Herbert Spencer, and of the so-called Manchester school of political economy. Its practical effects, which proceeded from the spirit of commerce and were largely anterior to the theory, aroused a lively indignation in writers like Carlyle and Ruskin, and indeed in all who were alive to the highest interests of our country. Its principle, stated briefly, was that government is in no way to interfere in the production or in the acquisition of wealth, but that its whole energy should be concentrated on the protection of wealth after it had been acquired. In the first of these aims it reproduced the political aspirations of the robber baron, who resents all interference on the part of a central government as prejudicial to his own line of business. I use the present tense, as many of that trade are still to be found in Anatolia and elsewhere. The important difference is, that whereas the robber chief is contented to rely for his protection on his own right arm, the princes of finance and commerce expect to have the whole strength of the community at their back. This arrangement is open to many objections. The one that concerns us here, is that, sooner or later, it leads inevitably to national disruption, and the consequent loss of national independence. The original justification both of law and of government, and what makes them preferable to anarchy, is that they protect the weak against the strong, and thereby produce freedom. Obscurity in the law, and the extreme liberty which is demanded by the school of *Laissez faire*, reverse the process. They add strength to the strong, and annihilate freedom. Their eventual result, if their operation is left unchecked, is a return to the anarchy of nihilism, or to what Rousseau calls a state of nature.

The first result of a commercial liberty which leaves the weak without protection against the strong is, as might have been expected, the rapid concentration of wealth in all branches of finance and commerce. The small shop gives way to the big store; the local banker is absorbed by the large centralized banking company; large farms take the place of *petite* culture; factories, of cottage industries; speculators in millions, of speculators in thousands; and so forth. The ultimate result is the growth of colossal fortunes in the hands either of corporations who, as such, have no conscience, or of individuals who, in the pursuit of wealth, are, and must be, in the same defective condition. For, as has justly been remarked, 'all the great prizes are for the unscrupulous.'[1] 'Large trading concerns beat smaller simply by their superior strength as fighting organizations.' A few of the unsatisfactory consequences of this tendency, as far as they affect freedom, must now be briefly indicated. The list does not pretend to be exhaustive.

In the first place a colossal fortune, in private hands, exposes a national government to the danger of corruption or intimidation. Public ends may be postponed to private interests. It is certain that the attempt will be made, and that in some cases, if not in all, it will be, eventually, successful. Government will be suspected, and will lose the confidence on which it depends for its influence with the people. Again, the power of wealth may make itself felt, without resort to the grosser forms of corruption, by its influence, mainly through the Press, on public opinion, and in a hundred other ways that elude detection. The

[1] Kidd, *Principles of Western Civilization*, p. 428.

effect will be disastrous to the authority of government, and, especially with a people which has always been impatient of control, to the cause of freedom.

The same danger threatens the economic development of a nation, by a double tendency, first, to supplant national by international interest; and, secondly, to erect a despotism within the nation, with power to defy the government. The great capitalist whose object it is to acquire money without regard to conscience or sentiment, and to whom patriotism makes no appeal (and this is the kind of being of which we are treating) will invest his capital in any country where it brings in the highest interest. His only concern with his own country will be to rely on its strength to support him in enterprises which may, in fact, have the effect of undermining the very strength on which he relies. His sympathies will be divided between the land of his birth and the land of his investments, whereas the former claims the whole. If he is a producer, his first aim will be cheapness of labour. He will find it in countries where the wants of the labourer are the simplest and the least highly developed; and competition will tend to reduce the position of labour in more civilized countries to the same low level. This, as has been pointed out, gives the black and yellow races an advantage over the white, and tends to reverse the course of civilization. Finally, the excessive disparity of fortunes is an outrage on justice, and sows the seeds of civil war.

The creation of a monopoly is the universal aspiration, or final end, of successful capitalism. It proceeds from the same mental characteristic, which allows no limits to dreams of conquest, and which forbids philosophers to be satisfied until they have reduced all the contents of their thought to a single universal principle: and it is ineradicable. A monopoly in any product or convenience which is essential to the well-being of the citizens is, so long as it is maintained, an independent power within the state, which the state, as has been shown by unsuccessful attempts in America, has not yet been able to cope with by peaceful methods. Private citizens are at its mercy, and, when the process has gone far enough, will cease to be free. It is a direct incentive to civil war.

The evil does not rest here. Freedom is the leading condition of evolution, the principle which makes progress possible. In stagnant communities, like China, the people may exist for centuries in a state of suspended animation, which cannot properly be called either freedom or slavery. But, where the spirit of progress is active, it inspires all classes of the community from the highest to the lowest, and none will submit to a life which excludes them from participation. It follows indeed, from our definition, that if they did the whole community in which they are citizens must lose its freedom, and cease to hold its place in the general advance of humanity. When, therefore, owing to the weakening of government through the principle of *laissez faire*, or for any other reason, the liberties of the powerful have gained so much ground as to invade the rightful liberties of the weak, the latter will, and ought to, resist with every means at their disposal. It is in the best interests of their country that they should. No community can attain its full strength when the free activities of the majority are unjustly curtailed.

It is in this aspect that the Revolution in France can be best understood. The people there, being unused to self-government or popular institutions, had recourse to brute force and bloodshed, and put themselves under leaders who were infected with Rousseau's views as to the advantages of a state of nature. In our own country they have adopted the forms of freedom, and organized themselves into unions, in which the personal interests of each individual are subordinated to the prosecution of an end which is common to all. This end is not the national end, but something quite different, and must often oppose it.

A trade union, when fully organized, may have

its definite number of members; its special rules or laws defining the liberties and responsibilities of each individual member; its sovereign government; and its common and clearly understood final end, which binds the members together in one community. It answers all the conditions of freedom; and may exercise more power, in proportion to its numbers, than a much larger body of men who are loosely bound together under a feeble government which is handicapped by an excess of liberty. It will differ from existing governments in two material points. In the first place, its criterion of membership will not be nationality, but occupation in some particular form of industry, and, secondly, its end will not be national, but following the general rule, a monopoly of power over all other classes of the community which are not included in the union. I may add here, as a probable conjecture, which, if right, is of great practical importance, that no such combination among the agricultural classes appears to be likely. They are too scattered to make it easy. At any rate they are not yet corrupted by the tendency. And, for both the political stability and the military power of any country, they are of greater value than any other class of labourer. Their occupation ensures both physical strength and hardihood of character,

The disadvantages of an industrial ideal are many. In the first place it will be restricted to the material needs of a particular class of individuals, who, from the nature of their work, can never be highly educated. A national ideal embraces the needs of all classes, and, even when predominantly material, must contain elements of a higher order. Again, their mere numbers make workmen more formidable than capitalists. If it comes to the worst, a dozen millionaires can easily be disposed of, but one firing party will be of no use against a million workmen. And it is not to be supposed that the many, when in pursuit of a low material end, will show themselves less deaf than the few have been to the dictates of conscience and humanity, or less blind to their own ulterior interests. They will not be withheld either by patriotism or by the certainty of their own eventual ruin from yielding to the temptation of a small temporary gain.

One of the principal dangers of unchecked capitalism, is, as we have seen, the internationalization of capital. An analogous danger arises, but in a worse form, from unchecked labour. Common action is only possible among men who have a common end, and when a particular class rejects the national end which binds together the rest of their countrymen, they must go for allies to men who are similarly situated elsewhere—that is to say, who have the same end as themselves, and a similar antagonism to the national end, whatever that may be, in other countries. This will undermine the national strength of all countries indifferently in which the disease has made serious progress, and will lay them open to subjugation by any other country, however barbarous, which is not infected to the same degree by the same disease. The internationalization of labour is indeed one of the most formidable of all the dangers which threaten our Western civilization, and it is the inevitable result of an unjust distribution of liberty.

It is obvious that the same consideration, in a modified form, applies to conflicts between separate nationalities within the complex of the same civilization. That country will have the best chance of success in which the principle of industrial selfishness exercises the least influence; and, if the conjecture which was hazarded a few pages back be justified, the total strength of each country will be largely dependent on the relative strength of its agricultural interest, when compared with the strength of all other forms of labour put together.

It is as well to repeat that when a war is over, and the country, which owed its defeat to the prevalence of industrial selfishness, lies under the heel of a more healthy conqueror, it will avail nothing to the conquered to appeal to the sentiment of industrial fraternity. That will count for nothing against the national sentiment of an enemy inflamed by victory. The result will be the same to the vanquished, whether the type of civilization which goes under be national or international. The class which contributed to its downfall will be buried under the ruins—an inglorious Samson, whose strength has been used, not against his enemies, but in their favour, and against his own compatriots.

Many more illustrations might be added of the effects of excessive liberty in the pursuit of the profits of trade. It may reasonably be supposed that a complete political equality between women and men, by annulling the most ancient and the most deeply-seated form of division of labour, would be a source of extreme weakness in any nation which adopted it. But the demand is inevitable (it is useless to ask whether it is justified) by the heartless and scandalous conditions of female labour, when capital is allowed to suck dry the life-blood of helpless women. Disloyalty to the state is the certain reaction when, under the shield of freedom of contract, the landlord imposes his own terms on an ignorant and helpless tenantry. The same result may follow if the principle of *caveat emptor* is held to justify another trade in poisoning the drink of the helpless labourer. In all these cases, and in many more, the state abdicates its function as the protector of the weak against the strong; it suffers its own authority to be undermined, and freedom is destroyed by liberty.

One more observation will conclude our remarks on this section of the subject. Weakness in a government breeds further weakness. What distinguishes a workman from an amateur is the sense of responsibility. No man can feel responsible for what he knows it is impossible for him to perform. When the strength of a government has been sapped by the inroads of liberty, it becomes aware that it no longer has the power to discharge its duties, and its action becomes feeble and amateurish. It will shrink from the employment of coercion. An efficient administration of the resources of a nation is one of the most valuable of the products of civilization, and a nation which is without it is as little likely to prevail against one which has it as the Aztecs were against the Spaniards. It has always been the habit of democracies when things go ill to blame their leaders, and they sometimes go the length of tearing them to pieces. But, if they will neither fight of their own will, nor submit to coercion, how are their leaders responsible? Let the people accept the blame, and reform themselves, instead of wasting a childish indignation on their own puppets. Let

TO NATIONAL GOVERNMENT 77

them learn the habit of obedience, and they will soon find a leader.

Need of Reform

That the degeneration of a nation follows close on its prosperity is perhaps the only sequence in historical events which approaches the certainty of scientific law. In Rome, the leading symptoms were the impotence of the senate and the degeneracy of the urban population; and the cause, an influx of material wealth, which removed all healthy restraint on self-indulgence.

Excessive liberty brought about the loss of freedom. With us, the consummation has not yet been reached. Our safety, so far, has been due to the survival in sufficient strength of the military virtues of patriotism and discipline. Early in the war some alarm may have been justified by the professions and attitude of the working-classes. But they were more than vindicated by the result. Their conduct in the field showed that they had lost nothing of the military virtues of their ancestors, or were at all inferior in courage or in endurance to the soldiers of Henry V. Any initial reluctance was probably not greater than would have been felt by any people to whose free choice it had been left to serve abroad against the German, or to stay at home. The war has taught us that it would be a senseless insult to compare the English workmen with a Roman mob.

Peace brings us face to face with another and, perhaps, severer trial. We find ourselves at the last stage of a long struggle between the conflicting principles of equality and inequality, that is to say, between the force of numbers and the force of eminence. Unless both of these are represented in its Government, if only by public opinion, no state can be free, and without freedom no nation can grow, or make progress. Of the two principles the moral sense of mankind awards the first place to equality; but it is also certain that eminence must be encouraged and rewarded; and this cannot be secured without a share of power. Numbers are nearer now than they ever were before to predominance. We may hope with some confidence that neither will their victory be complete, and merit be merged in a level flood, nor may their advance be thrown back by a force of eminence so base as that of Capital.

Nevertheless, no disinterested observer can be blind to the numerous symptoms of degeneration which mark the present course of our commercial civilization, or to their rapid growth on both sides of the Atlantic. Self-indulgence, with all its attendant vices, has sapped the strength and lowered the ideals at every large centre of trade

NEED OF REFORM

and industry, and in every grade of society: the government has no longer the strength it requires either for efficient internal administration or for the full organization of its resources against foreign enemies. Among the labouring classes, disruptive forces have appeared, which menace the national unity, and are obviously capable of involving the whole community in irretrievable disaster; while, from the opposite end of the social scale, Capital is apt to put gain before country, and an insincere literary philosophy, too timid to look fact in the face, and too soft to accept the fatigues and the sacrifices of patriotism, renders the same service to our enemies by discrediting our faith in national ideals. All these evils (and the list might be prolonged) are due to inordinate craving for liberty, and, unless that is counteracted, they will certainly increase.

Practical proposals to this end must be prepared to encounter a double difficulty. Retrenchment of liberty is always unpopular, and more than ever when the habit of self-indulgence has become inveterate. Again, democracies are not less greedy of flattery than despots are, or more likely to take in good part any indication of their defects. A writer who ventures to point them out, or a statesman who proposes to cure them, may count on an unfriendly reception. Nevertheless, the healthiest man is liable to smallpox, and a powerful physique does not make it wise to refuse to be vaccinated. Finally, it should be borne in mind that the intention of this essay is to deal with general principles which are valid for all forms of civilization, and that any references which may seem to be concrete are used chiefly as illustrations, and not as proofs. Any or all of them may be called in question without materially affecting the value of the argument as a whole.

Remedies

It remains then to inquire whether there is any remedy which ought to be adopted by all countries, in both hemispheres, when they are threatened, through excessive liberty, with national disruption. It seems evident that little can be expected from special measures directed to the redress of particular abuses. Unless the prevailing atmosphere, which favours nothing but liberty, is altered, they will soon cease to work, and fall into neglect. They would share the fate of Arctic vegetation transplanted to the tropics. The essential preliminary to all successful treatment is a change in the atmosphere; that is, a change in the national character. To that end there is only one means— that is a change in the national education. If the new element which is introduced in the national education is in harmony with older tendencies, which, though at one time powerful, have suffered a temporary set-back, the change should be easy. A language which it took years to acquire may be recollected in a few days.

No doubt can be left as to the direction which the change should take. When freedom is threatened with destruction through an excess of liberty, the remedy is not to reduce the love of liberty to what might be called a golden mean, but to supplement it by a fervent love of law. One of the most important functions of freedom, we may recollect, is the production of power for the defence of the national ideal against foreign aggression; and a nation would be in a bad way if for that purpose it had nothing to its credit but a lukewarm affection for liberty. What it requires is a passion for liberty, controlled and directed by a respect for law. A respect for law can only be gained by discipline, and discipline can never be too strict so long as it leaves the love of liberty intact, and confines itself to the task of checking its corruptions, and holding it firmly to the pursuit of the most elevated ends.

Again the strength of a nation is drawn from two opposite sources—commerce, and military power; and it may be attacked either through its commerce, or, more obviously, by arms. It must be prepared to defend itself against all forms of aggression. Of these, military force is certainly not the least dangerous; and, in order to repel this danger, it is the duty of every nation to maintain its own military power at the highest attainable degree of efficiency, without at the same time impairing the strength which it derives from its commerce. The spirit of commerce is allied with liberty; the military spirit with law, or discipline: and here again the all-pervading rule of strength holds good. Of the two opposed principles, you cannot keep one and reject the other. You must either keep both or lose both. The best type of citizen is not either the soldier or the civilian, but the civilian-soldier.

Finally, a nation can exert its full strength only when it is united in the pursuit of a common end. The end of commerce, as we have seen, is material wealth, and the effect of that is not to unite but to divide. Every man who pursues that end fights for his own hand, and, in the heat of conflict, loses sight of all the higher considerations of morality which bind men together as a nation. Devotion to material wealth can only be counteracted by setting up by its side some opposed end which is not material; and the ethical alternative is patriotism. Patriotism implies the readiness to sacrifice all material ends; it is directly opposed to the spirit of commerce, and it is one of the distinctive virtues of the military spirit. To a

REMEDIES

generation which has been accustomed to regard the accumulation of wealth as the sole criterion of success, such counsels may seem absurd; but the teaching of history is plain; and in that school there is no third choice; you must either learn, or be flogged. What kind of a flogging it is, Poland can tell. It compares with a school punishment as a battle-field does with a cricket match.

On three independent grounds the military spirit is absolutely essential as an ingredient in the national character of every commercial state:—

(1) As a curb on the unbridled love of liberty, which, by undermining the respect for law and order, exposes the state to internal disintegration, and consequent ruin.

(2) As a source of the military strength which is required for the protection of commerce.

(3) For the support of an elevated spiritual end, which unites all the citizens in a common cause, against the competition of selfish material ends which divide them. Of the two, liberty must always take the lead. We desire law as the means to liberty; not liberty as the means to law: and, in accepting law, we sacrifice a part of our liberty to freedom.

The military spirit can only be maintained by a military education, and, in order to make that education effectual, two conditions are indispensable—it must be universal, and it must be sincere.

A resort to ballot for filling the ranks leaves the liability to service universal; but it is objectionable in principle, because it fails to employ the whole of the nation's military strength. And this, I believe, can never be justified. The alternative is what is called the voluntary system. This offends against the conception of freedom we are now advocating in many ways. First, like the ballot, it leaves the nation at below its full strength. Again, instead of unifying, it divides the citizens into two classes, the civil and the military, with opposed ideals. If the army is small, it is useless, if it is large, it will overpower the civil element, and subordinate the aims of commerce to its own. This is the real danger of 'militarism'—a danger which may be safely neglected in a democracy, where every man is both civilian and soldier in his own person. Finally, a large standing army, though it no doubt will have military aims, will not prosecute them in the true spirit of a citizen soldier. Its spirit will be still, in the main, commercial. However patriotic the individual soldiers may be, the inducement which made them join the ranks, and keeps them there, is their pay. They dispose of their services in the open market, and do not give them, like the Spartans at Thermopylae, in obedience to

REMEDIES

the command of their people. Voluntary service has too strong an infusion of the commercial spirit to furnish an effectual antidote to commercialism.

The danger of insincerity is very real in a country where the sense of responsibility has been sapped by a permanent want of power on the part of the government to enforce its own orders, and where nearly everything, except the pursuit of money, is conducted in the spirit of an amateur. The discipline we require is not that of the half holiday or the picnic, but a severe training in spade work and long marches, and all else that may qualify a man to take part in immediate service in the field. Less than this will not avail us against an enemy who is vigilant and better prepared.

INTERNATIONAL FREEDOM

INTERNATIONAL FREEDOM

It has been observed at an earlier stage in this inquiry that freedom is a term which is not properly applicable to the human race as a whole, but only to individuals as communities of impulses, and to nations as communities of individuals. But, though that appeared to be a good reason for postponing the consideration of universal ends, or universal laws of morality, the treatment of the subject as a whole would be incomplete and unsatisfactory if all reference to a possible extension of freedom, beyond the fields in which it has already been realized, were omitted. A few lines must be added about the meaning and the practical requirements of universal freedom.

If the idea of freedom is to be raised to a higher level, it must be extended to the relations between nation and nation; nations being, at the present stage of evolution, the only units which intervene between individual men and humanity as a whole. From national or political freedom, the next step should be to international freedom. In order to realize the idea of international freedom it would be necessary, first, that nations should be united in the prosecution of an end which is common to all of them; secondly, that they should be ready to make national sacrifices towards the attainment of that end; and, finally, that they should acknowledge the presidency of a sovereign authority, which should determine the amount and nature of the sacrifice, and be in a position to enforce its own orders.

The only final end which is common to the whole of humanity, when regarded as a collective unit, is advance to a higher level of civilization; and this end can only be attained by an observance of the laws of morality. It would seem to follow, as a logical consequence, that if all men could be induced to submit themselves, without reservation, to the full law of morality, they would at once attain the ethical purpose of the race. But this would be a mistake. The consequence would be the extinction of morality; for it is quite certain that morality is wholly dependent on conflict, and if all men were of one mind there would be no conflict. Without evil, there would be no good. This is as true in conditions of stagnation as in conditions of progress. Even the most stagnant society is dependent for its existence on the observance by its members of the rules of morality. The universal extinction of conflict, and of the morality which is its necessary condition, is a pure fancy, such as no man of sense would care to waste thought on.

Stagnant civilizations—that is to say, communities which are held together by rules of morality, but exhibit no visible signs of progress—are extremely common. They constitute, indeed, by far the larger section of humanity, and there is no apparent reason, except a faith in the future, which itself has no base in reason, why they should not eventually embrace the whole of humanity. But these conditions, were they ever realized, would completely defeat the final end of humanity as a whole; that end being not merely existence, but advance to a higher level. Existence by itself, independently of the use which is made of it, is of a low value, or none at all.

The element in morality which saves us from stagnation, and secures our advance to a higher level, is freedom. Civilizations which are free are progressive, those which are unfree are stagnant; and freedom consists in the proper adjustment of the conflicting claims of liberty and constraint. If humanity as a whole is to advance, it must be guided by the retention of the same compromise among the community of nations. So long as individual nations are at liberty to pursue, each its own end, subject to the constraint of the laws of morality, so long will the whole community of nations to which they belong enjoy freedom, and be capable of progress; but no longer.

The principle of international freedom has been explicitly rejected by one of the principals in the present conflict, Germany by her representative thought proclaims, and in her collective action enforces, the doctrine that in conflicts between nations each party enjoys complete liberty of action, untrammelled by any moral considerations whatever. This amounts to a restatement of Rousseau's fundamental principle of complete liberty, and a return to a state of nature; but the application this time is to nations, instead of to individuals. If law is essential to progress, the necessary implication of this doctrine is that evolution stops with nations, and that beyond national progress there is no possible progress of humanity as a whole. In consonance with the same principle which explains the advocacy by capitalists of the doctrines of free trade and free contract, so, in the present case, the repudiation of the moral law emanates from the people which believes itself to be the strongest, and is directed against the liberties of the weak.

It remains to add a few words, first as to the nature and limits of any possible international law, and finally as to the means by which it may be enforced. It is quite certain that the law which regulates the practice of war among nations cannot be identical with the moral law which regulates the intercourse between individuals during peace. The moral law itself is not fundamental, but derivative from the law of the individual conscience; but consciences are not all alike, and the commands of the conscience of a single person may be, and often are, in conflict with the law of public morality. It is not therefore surprising if, in the same way, the law of international freedom should differ materially from the moral law of political freedom. It will be a more remote derivative from the commands of the general conscience, which contain the germs of all ethical law whatever.

For instance, to take human life, in a private quarrel, is only justified to the consciences of a great majority among ourselves by an immediate danger to life which there are no other means of repelling. In this case there is no necessary reference to the moral responsibility of the assailant, and no tribunal to decide as to the necessity. In the next higher stage, that is to say when the offence is against the community, life will not be taken unless moral responsibility on the part of the criminal is proved before a tribunal which is itself responsible. In both cases the fundamental justification is the same—that is, the preservation of life, first of the individual and secondly, of the community with its national ideal; but the conditions will be different, and, with them, the means of defence. In the case of the moral law when it is enforced by the state a new element is introduced; that is, moral responsibility on both sides of the transaction: of the offender on one side, and of the tribunal, as representative of the community, on the other.

The fundamental aim of international law is, in the same way, the preservation of life, but in this case it will be raised to a higher level. It will no longer be the life of the individual or the life of the community which is to be protected, but the life, under conditions of freedom, of the whole of the human race.

These considerations are applicable to stagnant communities, or to stagnant conditions of life over the whole human race. Men cannot exist except in communities, nor can a community exist without a moral law; but it is quite conceivable, and, on the analogy of other lines of evolution, not even improbable, that the human race as a whole may exhaust its power of evolution and stop short as a community, or number of separate communities, like those of bees or ants. In that case there might, perhaps, be no war; but, with the cessation of evolution, there would be no freedom: for the whole purpose of freedom is to enable men to rise to a higher level. The frustration of that purpose would be the greatest calamity that could befall the human race. It would mean the extinction of all their higher aspirations, and of everything in life that they now regard as really valuable. Morality itself will be transformed, and become a lifeless code of rules like the rules which govern a swarm of bees.

War, therefore, though not a good in itself, is the highest expression of that conflict between good and evil which is the universal and necessary form in which the course of evolution runs. The recognition of this truth supplies us with a basis on which we may define, with some reasonable prospect of success, the aims which should inspire a law of nations, which has for its final end the further evolution of the human race as a whole.

The first deduction is that the primary aim of international law will not be the suppression of war. In the first place, no sane man, reviewing the present condition of mankind, will believe that to be possible; and the commands of a tribunal which aims at an obvious impossibility will not inspire respect. In the second place, it is not even desirable. Its realization would mean the downfall of civilization through the rank growth of the vices of peace. What, then, should the aim be? The answer, when once given, is clear and certain.

The object of an international tribunal must be to exert its whole influence on the side of the good principle in its conflict with the principle of evil. No one is likely to object to this as impossible, still less as undesirable.

A few words of explanation may be useful. The conflict between good and evil in this life is the conflict between progress in evolution on one side, and on the other the sum of the forces which oppose evolution, and impose on the human race either stagnation, or, not impossibly, extinction. The maintenance of progress is not merely the most difficult task which the race has to cope with: it sums up the whole of its difficulties. Decay sets in directly the effort is relaxed. But, on the other hand, it is easy to go downhill. And as, in the case of a national state, no grain of power can be spared for the maintenance of its national freedom; or, in the case of an individual, moral freedom can only be attained and preserved by his exercise of the utmost resolution and vigilance: so, in the case of humanity at large, progress can only be maintained by throwing on the right side of the balance every grain of the power which it has at its disposal. It will be a strong reinforcement to the cause of good, if humanity can assert a collective adhesion to the principles of goodness, and support them when they are attacked. And it is unable to dispense with even the smallest grain of power which may be employed for its protection, but demands all that can be derived from every source. The absence of international law, well informed and properly directed, would mean the loss of freedom and the cessation of progress.

The initial aim, then, of international legislation is not the suppression of war, but the maintenance of peace. And there is no fear that, in the prosecution of this aim, it will achieve a suicidal success. The propensity to war is so strong, and the occasions of gratifying it so frequent, that it will be fortunate if it secures sufficient intervals of peace for the cultivation of the arts of civilization. So much, indeed, it would be reasonable to hope for, but only if it confined its intervention to cases in which there was some prospect of its being successful. When the national existence of one or both of the combatants was at stake, it would not be listened to, and its authority would be discredited.

This limitation does not apply, or at any rate not with the same force, within the next field in which international morality can and ought to exert its influence. Within war itself, the motives which are called in play are of every rank in the scale of morality, and range from the most sublime heights of heroism to the lowest depths of depravity. Again, the methods or implements employed vary greatly in their degree of destructiveness. On both these points, I believe, international law may intervene effectively, and, if it can, it is certainly in the interest of humanity at large that it should.

There is practically no limit to what may be written on this subject; but I must confine my observations to one branch only, without pretending to exhaust even that. It is urged that moral force is of equal value with military force, and that nations may be conquered by breaking their spirit as well as by defeating their armies; and it can hardly be denied that both of these methods combined are stronger than one by itself. The right to employ both, and to push each to its furthest limit, will be asserted by the nation which claims complete liberty, or emancipation from law—that is, by the strongest, or the one which believes itself to be the strongest. The claim will extend to the employment of means against combatants and non-combatants alike, which are degrading to the character of the men who resort to them, or which are such as to threaten the ultimate extinction of the race.

The opposed nation either may retaliate, or, preferring its honour to its existence, it may refrain. In the latter case it will fight against serious odds, and, if at the start it is the weaker, it will be likely to succumb. Whether it be right for a nation to accept martyrdom in defence of its national ideal may be debated : there are many who would think it should. In that case it would probably be defeated, and the higher ideal would be sacrificed to the lower, to the disadvantage of all the world. Or it may elect to retaliate by accepting the enemy's methods. In this case its own character would deteriorate; and again there would be an extension of evil. The result to humanity at large would be the same.

The investigation of the methods and principles of international law is a special subject. We need only add that it seems certain that there must be a tribunal with a final authority to enact rules; to decide questions which arise under them; and to enforce obedience to its orders. How that tribunal is to be constituted is a question on which, at present, it would seem premature to pronounce a definite conclusion. The whole subject is in its infancy, and we must wait for further experience. That the decision through natural evolution may take a wholly unexpected form is suggested by the fact that only a few centuries have elapsed since when the Pope occupied something very like that position in Western Europe, and enforced his orders by spiritual penalties. In our times we rely on voluntary co-operation between nations for the enactment of the rules, and on little more reliable than voluntary submission for the execution of the orders. This stage is evidently rudimentary and precarious, and the vital interests of mankind as a whole, demand that the constitution of the tribunal should be more intelligibly defined, and its powers very greatly enlarged.

Towards the latter object the expedient most frequently suggested is outlawry from the comity of nations. Outlawry is merely a translation of the word excommunication, and the two measures, though not the same, are closely analogous. Where they differ, the advantage is, I think, on the side of the spiritual weapon. The penalties of excommunication, or interdict, were religious, and, in an age of faith, they were invested with a force such as now we are hardly able to realize. The sufferings of every class in the Empire, and especially of the poorer classes, during the worst periods of the struggle between the Pope and the Emperor, were intense, and comparable to the ravages of a famine, or of a hostile occupation. And there was no counter effect on the authority which inflicted them. To the Pope and his subjects it was a matter of indifference whether the Germans were eternally saved or not, and it cost them nothing to maintain the excommunication as long as it was required. Outlawry from the comity of nations affects the outlaw mainly in his commercial relations; it is not likely to cause him great unhappiness; and the measure may react in a serious loss of wealth for the authority which imposes it. It is not therefore likely to be maintained for long. Where spiritual outlawry failed, commercial outlawry is not likely to succeed. Nevertheless, it is not necessary to deny that it might have a certain measure of influence.

The question, however, is not whether international law has any influence at all, but whether it has all the influence which it is possible to invest it with. In the defence of human freedom, it would be criminal to neglect any available source of strength. It must be remembered that they who assert perfect liberty and reject the restraint of the moral law are always that section within a community which is, or believes itself to be, the strongest. The function of law is the same throughout every stage of social development. In the association of impulses which makes up an individual, it protects the weaker and more lately developed among them against the furious passions which are inherited from the savage: in the association of individuals which makes up a nation, it protects the weaker and poorer classes against the robber baron and the landlord or capitalist; or, again, in a later stage, the few who are eminent above their fellows against the greed and envy of the masses; so, in the association of nations which make up mankind, it protects the freedom of the weaker against the tyranny of the strong. Further, we must remember that the function is continuous and interdependent throughout each of the successive stages. There can be no free nations without free men, and no freedom for humanity as a whole without free nations; nor, again, if we descend the scale, can there be any free men without freedom for humanity at large. The highest interests of every individual and every nation are inextricably involved in international freedom, that is to say, in maintenance of international law. That is the vital concern of all alike; and the assailants will always be the strongest members in the community of nations. To be neutral in the defence of international law means to leave one's own most vital interests to the protection of that party in the conflict which will, presumably, be the weaker.

Now, military force, though not the only source of strength, is probably the most valuable of all; and, if the elevating effects of military experience, both during preparation and in the field, be taken into account, it is certainly indispensable. Any nation which neglects this, and fails to keep it at the highest possible point of efficiency, sacrifices a large portion of its possible strength, and is unfaithful both to itself and to humanity at large. Moreover, the unrestricted growth of the commercial vices of luxury, sloth, and dishonesty will speedily undermine its strength, even in the realm of commerce. Finally, the pursuit of material wealth will ensure, sooner or later, its political disruption. It will become a negligible quantity, and its voice will cease to be listened to in the council of nations. The sacrifice which is entailed by the maintenance of a national army will not really be greater than what is imperatively demanded for the preservation of national independence, or indeed of freedom in any of the stages of its evolution. The cause of righteousness is one and indivisible, and has no use either for an economy of means or for a calculated devotion.

Either all must be armed or none. A small army has no better chance than a mediocre poet. If one nation arms, all the rest must follow, in order to keep that one quiet; if one remains disarmed, nature will assert her rights, and it will be partitioned among its wiser neighbours. The foolish virgin will find no friends to help her. As soon as there are more armies than one, competition will set in, and, for the same reasons which started it, it will not cease until each and all of them have attained their utmost limit of strength.

Even for its internal preservation every nation must have its army, though for that purpose only it need not, perhaps, be a large one. Arms can be bought by the citizens; internal crises will arise in which an unarmed police will be useless; and government will be paralysed. Put arms in the hand of a single policeman, and in the course of a very few years you must have a nation in arms. To suppose that peace may be maintained without preparation for war, or that the effort need be less than the utmost that all the associated nations are capable of, is a delusion. The offender will always be confident in his own strength, and the protests of unarmed peacemakers will have no more effect than the bleating of sheep or the angry demonstrations of a flock of geese.

BOOK II

LIBERTY

LIBERTY

MORALITY

Καὶ μὴν ὁ χρησμὸς οὐκέτ' ἐκ καλυμμάτων
ἔσται δεδορκώς.
Aesch. Ag. 1178–9.

Color che ragionando andaro al fondo
S'accorser d'esta innata libertate;
Però moralità lasciaro al mondo.
Dante, Purg. xviii. 67–69.

In spite of ardent efforts, thinkers have not yet succeeded in elaborating on a monistic basis any theory of ethics that is satisfactory and answers to the deepest needs of man. Nor will they succeed.
A. Harnack, What is Christianity?
3rd. ed., p. 153.

LIBERTY

MORALITY

Introductory

IN my essay on 'Freedom' I made the following contrast between the aim or final end of religion and the aim of freedom. 'In the religion which we profess the final end is placed in another world, and is gained by entry into a new life in which all ends of this life are rejected as devoid of independent value. With this aim freedom has no concern whatever. The aims of freedom are confined to this world, and do not look beyond it. They are advance in civilization. The whole scale of its values lies between the life of a savage and the life of a Michael Angelo; between the institutions of Dahomey and those of Great Britain. Its sole aim in the future is to increase that difference. The aims of religion, on the other hand, have no reference to evolution. The soul of a Michael Angelo is of no higher value to it than the soul of a naked savage. For religion all interest centres in the individual soul' (pp. 10, 11). The end of Morality not being identical with that of religion, being, indeed, directly opposed to it, and the end of freedom being identical with that of morality, I proceeded to discuss, in what was a purely moral treatise, the moral form of freedom, without anything more than a passing notice of religion.

This, however, was clearly inadequate for an ethical treatise, and afforded by itself no safe guide to conduct. The object of ethics is the discovery of a complete system of conduct, and no system which deals with movements is complete unless it is furnished with a final end—a *terminus ad quem*. Without a final end freedom may realize itself instinctively, and flourish for a short time; but if it adopts a wrong final end it chooses a wrong path and is lost. That the conscience, which supplies the forms of freedom, supplied no final end of conduct I clearly stated on the same page: 'The conscience has no ends of its own—the essential character of its commands is that they must be obeyed without regard to consequences.' On the same page I urged that Greek philosophy, being based exclusively on past experience, is fatal to adaptation, as it defeats, instead of promoting, the ends of freedom, which are new and unknown, and unlike and beyond all past experience. Where then are we to discover our ethical final end? If we trust to morality itself we obtain an answer which is not unlike the religion of Manes. The conflict between good and evil will continue as long as the world endures. Morality cannot go beyond itself, and does not, by giving itself a religious form, acquire any new knowledge unless it derives it from the religion itself.

Again, the sole aim of morality is to promote growth. And all law is derived, eventually, from the conscience. Morality, or the codified commands of the conscience, provides the universal type of law. Now, what makes good law is justice, and justice is equality between conflicting claims. Strict justice excludes the emotions. It is admitted that to admit love or hatred in questions of justice deflects the judgement. It has no reason for declaring a preference between love and hate themselves. In its own operations it is consciously averse to both. In order that the conscience may enlist the support of the whole human nature it must require the intellect as a guide to point out its direction, and the emotions as a source of strength for attraction or repulsion. Attraction is love; repulsion hatred; or rather those are the respective emotions which are set up by the two tendencies; and a man who was weak in either emotion would fail in the tendency to which it was appropriate; if in both, he would fail altogether. The law excludes both from its own operations, but for its own decisions it demands from its subjects hatred for what it condemns, and love for what it approves. Between the conflicting emotions it maintains the same indifference as it does in the case of every other pair of opposites that is submitted to it.

A system of perfect indifference, in which each member, good or bad, in every pair of opposites is of equal value, annihilates growth. In fact, it destroys the distinction between good and evil, and with that morality itself. When a preference has been given to a single earthly end, history teaches us that there has been a slight forward movement, but that it has been almost immediately arrested, and has been followed by a rapid decay, and, with the rest of the civilization, its peculiar morality, to which it owed its growth, has also disappeared. The civilizations of Babylon and Memphis have fallen, and if any traces of them have survived it has been by adoption into a stronger form of life.

What then is the special feature of a morality which ensures its growth and preserves it from destruction? None remains for our choice except the adoption of a final end in another world which is above and beyond the range of our earthly experience, and the acceptance of that for our guidance. It will no more dream of reaching it than the sailor will hope to reach the North Star, but it will be saved from aimless wanderings on a pathless ocean, and the crew from eventual starvation. The aim of the sailor, though on another element, is known to him; it is in the same earth, and he and others

INTRODUCTORY

may have been there before, and have learned all that they wish to know about it. The goal of morality is one from which there is no return, and about which nothing can be known except by revelation. The function of morality may be compared to the seamanship which keeps the ship afloat and moving, but does not prescribe its destination.

It is to the further explanation of this thesis that the following essay is directed. A concrete application may be permitted at once. All use of force is opposed to perfect liberty and to the temper of love. It is therefore forbidden. If a man strikes you on the right cheek you must turn him the left. But it may be that in doing so you contradict the commands of your conscience by sacrificing your freedom, which can only be maintained by active resistance to forcible aggression. Freedom is necessary to growth; and the maintenance of growth is the highest of the moral duties. It can only be maintained by law, and law is constraint, or the exercise of force. So far then as force is necessary to the maintenance of freedom it is both justified and commanded by the conscience. When it is not necessary for that purpose it is abhorred and condemned. Wars of aggression are not directed to secure freedom, and are condemned, but whether a war is aggressive or defensive depends on the intention and not on the priority of inception. A war is aggressive if the intention of a nation in undertaking it is to destroy the freedom of its opponents and, in the case of victory, to substitute its own form of civilization for theirs, and it may begin as defensive but become, in the end, aggressive. Only in modern history do we find the repeated failure of all attempts at universal dominion, combined with the unbroken growth of single civilizations, and of a number of independent and conflicting national ideals. The prosecution of a war which respects the freedom of others, and demands every sacrifice for its maintenance, is the highest and most difficult exercise of the Christian spirit of love.

That such a final end actually existed, and what it was, did not occur to me till quite lately. The passage which is quoted at the beginning of this essay proves my ignorance, and that while I had worked out, with, I hope, a fair approach to completeness, the form of morality, I had failed to provide it with a final end, and that as a system of ethics my writings were still vitally defective. It then occurred to me that the defect was supplied by Christianity; the religion which the great majority of us profess and which, in one form or another, is accepted by all the most powerful nations in the world. Christianity teaches us that there is a divine supernatual end which cannot be reached in this life, but will be accorded to all true believers after death; and a Divine emotion which, in the same way, cannot be fully operative except in another world. The final end is perfect liberty or release from law; the Divine emotion is love. But for the government of the world in which we live morality must still remain as the sole guide of conduct: not, indeed, any kind of morality, but morality which is directed towards the heavenly end. Morality is, itself, law, and the temper of law is not love but justice, or the exclusion of both love and hatred. On the leading principle of equality, which constitutes justice, if love is admitted, hatred must be admitted in an equal degree. It is only by the declaration that all the ends of morality on earth are temporary, and that the only end that is real and absolute is beyond this world and above the ends of morality, that the law can be given a bias which will impart a steady direction to its guidance. A complete system of ethics is then a composition of a natural morality with a supernatural final end. An equally complete system would be furnished by a religion which, by making law or the absence of Liberty the supernatural condition, and hatred the Divine temper, reversed the order of the moral values. That would be devil worship. Manichaeism, as has just been remarked, adds no final end to morality.

The whole of this scheme has been deduced from a single assumption, namely, that evolution consists in the parallel progression of opposites; and that under any definition of good and evil, the growth of either has always been roughly counterbalanced by a nearly parallel growth of the other. It follows that if improvement means advance towards any conceivable ideal there is no such thing as improvement. All motion either radiates from a point or withdraws towards it in all directions. The ratio between the centripetal and centrifugal forces always remains practically the same, though their distances may vary. Morality has no final end. Its own business is that of justice, or the maintenance of a ratio of equality between conflicting principles. For its final end it has recourse to religion. If religion selects an ideal among the members of a pair of conflicting opposites, it interferes with the justice of Morality, and breaks up the mechanism of life. The aim of liberty on earth implies the destruction of law, and consequently of freedom. The aim of liberty beyond this life only affects the process of earthly life, that is the justice of morality, by giving it a bias in favour of liberty against law; but it is far from demanding the destruction of law, or any reduction of it beyond what would be dangerous to life. It is not unusual to claim a great improvement for the modern era when compared with antiquity, but it would not be easy to give reasons; still less to prove its permanence. There has been a very great increase in the element of liberty, but there has, perhaps, been an almost equally great increase in the growth of law: for the sake of freedom it may be hoped there has been. Again, it seems premature to boast that slavery has been finally abolished. As an institution it has only been quite recently made illegal, and, had the fortune of the late war been different, it might very well have been introduced in the mines in England. Again, Socialism is the extreme application of the Christian principle of human equality, and at the same time is directly opposed to the law of the Church. The reason is that its maintenance would call for a strictness of law that would destroy freedom and crush eminence. There are, further, very sound reasons for fearing that Socialism will not be maintained at all, unless slavery is introduced again for the less attractive industries, and the people distinguished between citizens and not citizens. The effect of Christianity on morals is not to destroy or even to weaken law in its relation to liberty, but to define their relative positions by making liberty the final end; and law the necessary means.

Liberty and Law

The sole object of our will, and the only original source of all we love and all we desire, is liberty. Liberty means the conditions under which action or life is perfectly free, independent, and untrammelled. Liberty then is universal life. And life is shown in action: without action of some kind (whether it be internal, and take the form of thought; or external, and take the form of aggression on, or resistance to, external forces) life is not recognized. We may then take life as the equivalent of action, and define liberty as the condition under which action of all kinds is perfectly exempt from restraint, and this, that is to say perfect liberty of action, is the sole and undivided object of the will. The two are barely distinguishable: we act because we will, and we will in order to act; they are inseparable. The product of perfect liberty on earth is license, or chaos. Life knows no moral distinctions; it is wholly indifferent to good and evil.

On the other hand, coeval with life and opposed to it is law. In the sense that inert matter is subject to natural law it may be said that law is anterior to life, and life may be represented as a rebellion against it. But, if the meaning of life be extended so as to cover all forms of evolution this distinction vanishes. All life, in the usual sense of the word, is organic; that is to say, subject to rule and order. It is the principle which gives form and order to all that we see and hear and know. It is not, however, the cause of evolution. Every new quality that presents itself to our knowledge represents a victory of life over law; but it is law that makes evolution possible, by attaching innovations to types which already exist and producing new types. That is to say, it adopts the material which is given it by life, and moulds it in a form which is given by itself. As opposed to life the operation of law is destructive. It arranges the changes which are due to life in classes, by cutting off those forms in which the internal principle of change is abnormal. It is the sole original cause of all that we hate and avoid. It enforces itself by penalties for disobedience; by disease and death. Life brings rewards, first pleasure, and then happiness: law, penalties; but law is the universal condition without which life cannot maintain itself on earth.

Law on earth is of two kinds, the scientific and the moral, and the second of these differs from the first in the point that it admits free will, whereas the other proceeds on the hypothesis of uniform sequence. Free will is the self-assertion of life independent of law, and the whole function of science is to reduce its manifestations in the past to the law of uniform sequence. This task it discharges with imperfect success, and every moment enlarges the bounds of its province by the addition of fresh matter from life. Of the future it can see nothing except so far as it resembles the past. The secrets of future growth are a sealed book to it. Science produces nothing new, διάνοια αὐτὴ οὐδὲν κινεῖ. The whole world of phenomena is the product of movement, and movement, even in inanimate nature, must be ascribed to a life which has not yet assumed the appearance of purpose. All the operations of life, in all stages, are in themselves spontaneous.

Though the universality of change compels us to assume the presence of life even in the smallest particle of matter, the change in the lower grades of phenomena which mark the evolution of the world is so slow as to be imperceptible, and for the purpose of science it is necessary to disregard it. Science deals with a universe which it regards as stationary in its present conditions of life. In a later stage change becomes so rapid that it suggests the conception of purpose. When a cell converts external matter into its own substance we ascribe a purpose to the process, and call it living. Later still, life becomes conscious and is aware of its own efforts. Finally, at its last stage, it develops the conscience, and is aware of the possibility of alternative courses of action in the same conditions, and of an independent principle which commands us to take one course and reject the other. We know that it is in our own power to adopt either of two courses which are offered to us, and either to obey or to disregard the commands of our conscience; and this power we call the freedom of the will. The separate commands of the conscience, when generalized, become the moral law, which is a vast collection of maxims unconnected by any single universal principle. The discovery of a single universal principle, by reference to which all the various maxims of morality may be connected and co-ordinated in a system of relative values, is the task of ethics. The universal connecting principle can be nothing but a final end or purpose.

There is a third form of law, which is not earthly in its origin, and which, therefore, is not within the range of philosophy. That is the Divine Law, or law of religion. The essential character of that law is that it continues the life of man beyond the grave; and subjects him to rewards and penalties in another world, on the judgement of God. The reward, according to the Christian religion, is perfect liberty in Heaven; the penalty, perfect slavery in Hell. All questions relating to the nature and meaning of its commandments are the province of Theology; their practical effect on conduct is within the cognizance of ethics, and forms the subject of this essay.

The Divine Law is the law of morality, when that has been supplemented by, and is guided in, the direction of a religious final end. When the moral law is directed towards an earthly final end the system is philosophic and not religious. All values, or rules of preference, are determined by a final end. There are values of glory, and values of pleasure, in which the final end is either power or pleasure; and there is the ethical final end, and the values of the conscience, whose guiding principle on earth is the growth of life. The last has no final end of its own.

Morality and Final End

The first article in our Ethical Creed is that the goodness of an action depends on the final end to which it is directed.

The second article is that the final end of life is life. By this is meant not more life, for that would be a process and not an end, but a state of perfect liberty, in which life acts quite independently and without restrictions.

This is a complete and, perhaps for individuals, not an impossible ideal. There may be men whose spirit is so imbued with the spirit of liberty as to become identified with it. Such men cannot go

MORALITY AND FINAL END 123

wrong, all their actions are right. But on the attainment of this stage two results are necessarily consequent.

1. No further advance is possible. *Neque nubent.* The perfect leave no progeny.

2. No inquiry into the laws of morality will be necessary. Such men have left law behind them when they attained liberty. An ethical philosophy will not only be superfluous but impossible.

The province of an ethical inquiry is the continued life of men on earth; and the universal feature of that life is evolution, or the regular change of life to more life, or to less life—a process, that is, of either increase or decrease of life; of growth or of decay. And the aim of morality is not absolute liberty but growth; that is to say, not life absolutely but increase of life. But we find that on earth the growth of life is strictly conditioned by law, and, primarily, by the law of morality. All such men whose will, or principle of action, is already in complete conformity with the spirit of life have no need of law. They are above morality and can work miracles. They have reached their end, and have no call for further growth. But few, if any, such men exist. All others, and they form practically the whole of the human race, are in a state of change, and for them law is indispensable. Their aim in life is not liberty but freedom.

It might be thought that the growth of life would correspond with the decay of law, and that perfect freedom would, in time, develop into perfect liberty. Liberty would then serve as the final end of morality, and might be realized in this world. For this view there is no justification in history. From the beginnings of life, growth in liberty has always been attended by growth of law, and there is no reason to suppose that the nature of the process will ever change, or that morality will ever abolish its own influence. Freedom demands law as certainly as it does liberty. Without law it ceases to be freedom and becomes chaos, or the absence of ordered life. And law and liberty arise at the same time; their growth is parallel; and at every stage of evolution their quantity (if the word quantity may be used in this connexion) must be about equal. The distance from zero will be nearly equal for both.

Growth means the equal increase of both life and law, and any material excess either of law or of life over the other brings about not merely cessation of growth but rapid decay. It is clear then that the universal criterion of morality is neither law nor liberty, but equality between the two. And the universal moral good is equality, or Justice; the universal moral evil is inequality or injustice. All evil is excess or defect; but not with any reference to any standard in the quality itself on which judge-

MORALITY AND FINAL END

ment is passed. The standard is the degree of development which has been reached at the same period by the other member in a pair of opposites. Excess in one of the pair and defect in the other are correlative terms: one necessarily involves the other. If there is too much liberty it is because there is too little law, and vice versa; and there is no other meaning to excess and defect. Justice alone, as the ratio between opposed qualities, has no opposite quality: it is purely mathematical.

Justice then, or the equal strength of opposed qualities, is the sole essential means to growth. Its value is not that of an end in itself, but as an indispensable condition of growth or of evolution. Evolution itself is not an end, but merely a process tending in a certain direction, which for reasonable comprehension requires to be furnished with an end. Morality acts in the support of growth, and the final end of morality must be the same thing as the final end of growth or of evolution. What then is the final end of evolution? This is the vital question of ethics, and without an answer it is impossible to construct a complete ethical system. The answer is not given by the conscience, which supplies our ideas of what is just. Nor does conscience get any help from science. To both the future of evolution is quite unknown. Both are completely ignorant not only of the final end of evolution but even as to its slightest movement in the immediate future : what it will be, and whether its direction will be in advance or in retreat. In the contest between liberty and law, which constitutes a free life on earth, no qualities are absolutely good or absolutely bad. Love of your neighbour is good, of your neighbour's wife is bad; hatred is bad, but Saul lost his kingdom and his life for the slackness of his hatred of the Amalekites. And the total destruction of the Amalekites may have been required for the survival of the religion of Israel, and eventually as a necessary step towards the redemption of the world.

What then is the universal end of human action? The answer is liberty. But it is a liberty which is in heaven and not on earth. To seek to realize it on earth breaks down the whole machine which has been erected throughout countless ages under the guidance of life by law. What then is the use of an end which no man may strive to realize on earth, except under the certain penalty of the abrogation of morality and the destruction of life itself? It is this. The knowledge that liberty is the real end of all action, and even of constraint itself, teaches man that his morality embraces two contradictory principles, one of which, that is liberty, can only be realized beyond this world, whereas the other, that is law, is entirely of this world; it teaches him that the first is the end and the second the means, and it enjoins on him, as his highest duty while he is on earth, to respect and obey the law so long as it is just, and to resist it by every means in his power when it is unjust. That liberty is not an earthly end; that, as long as the earth endures, law must always bear the same proportion to it as it does now, seems certain. 'Donec transeat caelum et terra, iota unum aut unus apex non praeteribit a lege, donec omnia fiant. Nisi abundaverit iustitia vestra plus quam Scribarum et Pharisaeorum, non intrabitis in regnum caelorum.'

How do we judge that any action or impulse is right or wrong, just or unjust? This is the most important practical question in ethics, and the most difficult to answer. It will be considered in a separate chapter. In the meantime it will be enough to say that the basis of all moral judgement is the conscience. But the conscience is no more the same in different individuals than the taste or the aesthetic judgements. In some men it is wide, in others it is narrow in comprehension; in some its reactions are strong, in others feeble; two men may judge differently on the same question. In order to provide a moral law, or general authority in moral questions, it becomes necessary to generalize the separate individual judgements; and in order to secure system and avoid contradictions the assumption of a final end is indispensable. This is beyond and outside of morality. The moral judgements disclose no general directions or end, but contrary directions: Justice itself is an equilibrium between opposites. Nor can it be found in natural science: to that, the future of evolution is a closed book. This is equally true of philosophy, which deals with the past and not with the future, and is unable to legislate for the future except on the hypothesis that nothing changes. Moreover it is found that any final end that may be placed within experience contradicts instead of correcting the moral judgements, and is followed by degeneration and not by growth. Any final end that is to connect the moral judgements and not involve them in contradictions must be placed beyond the limits of experience; and beyond experience philosophy cannot reach.

As a preliminary outline this will perhaps suffice. The evidence will follow. The whole practical teaching is this: that for the guidance of his conduct, including his thought, which is the most important branch of his conduct, a man must choose between his metaphysics and his morality. Metaphysics is bounded by experience. Morality demands a final end which is beyond experience. Metaphysics has always depreciated the study of final ends: and quite rightly. It is conscious of its incongruity with its own methods. One deals with the sequence of phenomena as determined by previous phenomena

MORALITY AND FINAL END

which it calls causes: the other is concerned with the actions of men as determined by ideals in the future. In baptizing the final end, or ideal, as the 'final cause', the Greeks attempted to reduce the latter to the same category as natural causes. But the two are wholly distinct both in subject as in method; and to apply the method of either to the subject of the other inevitably leads to disaster. There can be no science when ethical ends are admitted; and no moral development when thought is directed by the principle of uniform sequence.

Co-operation and Competition—Equality and Inequality

Growth is promoted either by co-operation or by competition. The earliest forms of life are single cells, which breed by fissure and may seem to enjoy a perfectly independent and eternal life, all losses being due to external accidents and not interfering with the main stream. But this view would be mistaken. It is found that after a certain number of births by fissure the original vigour of life fails to maintain itself, and must be restored by the union of two disconnected cells. At its lowest stage the indefinite prolongation of life is dependent on the co-operation of two different cells. Further progress along the same path is made when large numbers of cells coalesce in colonies, as sponges, plants, and animals. A further advance is made when the animals such as ants and bees, and other social forms of life, unite in hives and nests and packs for the common purpose of supporting life: or men, with the same purpose, combine in tribes or cities or nations. And co-operation does not stop there. It may grow to groups of nations, who suppress their separate interests in the pursuit of a single common end. The emotion which promotes co-operation is love; and the tendency self-sacrifice.

But conflict is at least as important to evolution as co-operation is. One of its main sources is competition, and particularly competition for the means of subsistence, that is to say for life itself. So impressive is the spectacle of its operation that the leading school of natural philosophers have selected it as the sole principle of evolution. We cannot stop to examine this view; but of the existence of the process in our own days there can be no shadow of doubt. All human life is engaged in an internecine struggle, between class and class, trade and trade, and nation and nation; to say nothing of the unremitting contest between man and external nature which expresses itself, among other results, in disease ; and of all orders of animals among themselves. The emotion which is born of conflict is hatred; the tendency, self-assertion.

EQUALITY AND INEQUALITY

Competition is the self-assertion of the strongest, and it is as necessary to growth or evolution as co-operation is.

Another conflicting pair of opposites, derived from the opposition between liberty and law, is this. From the point of view of liberty it is certainly true that all men are born equal. The end of liberty is the maintenance and increase of life, and this end is universal. To the bare right to exercise his powers for the prosecution of this aim every man, whatever his colour, or his mental development, or his social position may be, is equally entitled. It is for this reason that murder, or the malicious deprivation of life, is equally reprobated, whether the victim be young or old, white or black, rich or poor, noble or ill born. The radical equality of every man's right to pursue his own aims is reflected in the equality of all men before the law, and in the just hatred for slavery which is felt by every man who values either liberty or freedom.

On the other hand, it is equally true that men are born unequal, and that their inequality is not only a sign of a higher degree of life in the eminent, but also an indispensable condition of growth for the whole race. If all men were born the same, all would remain the same. No elevating education would do its work, or indeed could come into existence; for all elevation is the fruit of an elevated character.

It is for its services to the growth of human life that men have attached the concept of merit to superior excellence; and by merit they mean a title to a reward. If all men were exactly equal there could be neither merit nor reward. Inequality runs through all nature. No two grains of sand are exactly alike. And it is the keystone of evolution. If all were equal, selection would have no meaning. And all equality, without exception, is a difference in life, or in the power to grow. The sole superiority which possesses an ethical value is a higher evolution of life.

The reward which men pay to acknowledged superiority is admiration or glory. Glory must not be confused with goodness; for superiority may be used in either direction: it may pull down or it may raise up; whereas goodness is used only for action that raises up, and does not necessarily imply any other distinction. No one would call Charlemagne good; and it would be an interesting problem for a debating society to discuss which title should be preferred, Charles the Great or Louis the Saint. Nor should glory be identified with pleasure. Pleasure is an internal satisfaction which accompanies the successful achievement of any action, and it is undeniably more intense when the impulses which prompt it are of a lower or common order, such as the procreation of offspring or the satisfaction of hunger. Glory, on the contrary, is an external tribute which is paid by onlookers to distinction, and its greatness is in direct proportion to the height of the achievement; not, as pleasure often is, in the inverse proportion.

It is clear that the emotion which is proper to competition, whether for pleasure or for honour, is not love but hatred. The most universal and legitimate cause of hatred is insult; and insult is nothing else but the imputation to another of inferiority. Whether the imputation is true is quite immaterial; the form of insult becomes stereotyped, and often throws a curious light on the mental habits of the nation in which it is current. In Germany the conventional insult is to call a man stupid (*dummkopf*); in India, to assert the existence of conjugal relations with the ladies of the victim's family,[1] thereby implying a slight inferiority in his position on the social scale. In England the first might be thought uncivil; the second would not be understood. The resentment at the imputation of inferiority is intolerable. It is the parent of hatred, envy, and malice; and provoked the first murder. On the other hand, superiority, whether fancied or real, breeds insolence and contempt; but, with the reward it offers, it is at the root of all progress.

[1] *Sasur*, father-in-law.

Ideals

The ideals which are based on a combination of the mass of moral maxims with a definite reasonable end have been very numerous; and each constitutes in itself a complete system of morality. Thus we have, among many others, the various philosophic systems of the ancient world, with their modern representatives: the national systems of Athens and Sparta, of Rome and Carthage; and the conflicting national systems of modern Europe, which grew up from the new birth of classical ideas at the Renaissance, and which were at the root of our late war. None of these various ideals is, or can be, universal, though the aim of all people who enter on an aggressive war on the behalf of any one of them is to make their own universal by imposing it on all the people they can reach. The dream of universal dominion is explained by the passion to enforce universally that ethical system which is believed to be the sole source of life by the man who goes to war for it. And the glory he earns from success is paid to the nature of his attempt.

The solution which is offered by Christianity is to transfer the end of action from this world to another. It tells us that this world is under a curse, and all its ends are evil. The other world, in which the real ends of action are found, and on which all our action in this life should be concentrated, is beyond the reach of human reason, and is supernatural. It is in no way a continuation or an improvement of the existing state of things, but a new creation ; which will be introduced, not gradually, but very suddenly without warning, and after the total destruction of this creation. Entrance into it is determined by Divine selection, and not on any grounds that are intelligible to human reason. This is one-half of the doctrine. It makes no reference to morality, and, if it stood by itself, it would have little interest to an ethical philosopher. It would indeed make his task superfluous by annihilating morality. But it is only half, and it is supplemented by rules of conduct on earth, which are to be in force for the period while men are waiting for the advent of the new dispensation. The object of these rules is to keep alive the doctrine of the new creation until it arrives. Their repository is the Church on earth.

The ethical effect of Christianity has been to introduce a new and higher dichotomy in the radical principles of action. It collects all the various and conflicting earthly ideals of the ancient world in one class, and condemns all of them as evil; opposing to them, as good, its own ideal of perfect liberty in another world after death. But it retains the laws of the conscience for the guidance of conduct on earth, re-arranging them in a new order of precedence with regard to their relative value in promoting the attainment of the new supernatural ideal. It sharply distinguishes between this life and the next, and makes the next the end of this, and the criterion of our actions. Of that world reason tells us nothing: we must accept it on faith.

The Christian ideal will never be more nearly approached in this world than it is already, and always has been. Until the day of judgement the tares will grow with the wheat: to destroy the weeds will at the same time destroy the whole crop. All that the Church, or Christ's kingdom on earth, can effect is to maintain the growth of the principles of the Heavenly Kingdom as against those of the world, and secure them the first place. If it asserted the possibility that its own principles might be realized on earth, it would add another to the Pagan philosophies, and destroy the growth by depressing unduly one of the two opposite principles. It would set about the impossible task of weeding out the tares. To keep the wheat above the tares, though difficult, is not hopeless. It is the struggle between the new man and the old, which for most of us is not decided in this life.

The most fundamental of the changes made by Christianity was the transposition of the relative values of law and liberty. In the estimation of the ancient world, law unquestionably took the leading place among these two conflicting concepts ; but the value of liberty was not overlooked. The Jewish morality was probably the highest of all, when judged on abstract grounds, as it certainly was the nearest in its approach to Christian morality; but, in that, the pre-eminence of the law was decided, and increasing. In the centuries between the captivity and the birth of our religion prophecy had been nearly silent, or had been absorbed in eschatological speculations which had little or no bearing on daily life. The rule of law was every day becoming more severe and more minute. In earlier ages the prophets had asserted liberty ; but it was liberty in the service of the law, and its aim was the further evolution of the law. Among the Greeks, and the Romans also, law certainly stood highest. As Lord Acton remarks (*History of Freedom*, p. 16), ' The ancients understood the regulation of power better than the regulation of liberty ' ; and that was because law held the first place in their thoughts. But in two at least of their peoples the idea of liberty glowed with special life. One of them erred by restricting its enjoyment to itself and refusing participation to its subjects and its allies, but it has left us an unequalled treasure in art, and in thought, and in literature ; the other conquered the world, and it bequeathed to posterity nearly all that is valuable in the concepts of law : but in extinguishing rival moralities it extinguished growth. The same result ensued on the conquests of Alexander, and no doubt would have followed the success of Athens had she imposed and maintained her own dominion. In Christianity, on the contrary, liberty takes the first place, and law is only valued as an instrument for the protection and further growth of liberty.

The Jews were probably, under their theocratic government, the people who, of all ancient nations, gave the most complete effect to the principle of human equality. But, even among themselves, they recognized the division between the priest and the people, of which the former succeeded to their rank by heredity and formed a real aristocracy. Outside their own polity lay the whole heathen world to whom they denied all rights, and whom they rigidly debarred from community of bed and board. Christianity, in abolishing for Gentiles the validity of the Mosaic Law, destroyed, first, the distinction between priest and layman, and then the distinction between Jew and Greek. All men were the children of the same Heavenly Father and absolutely equal. A more unreserved statement of the principles, within the Church, of complete human equality could not be conceived. Nevertheless, in its contact with the world, the Church restored the Jewish distinctions between priest and layman, and between believer and unbeliever. On the other hand, the influence of the principle of human equality made the appointment to the priesthood elective instead of hereditary, and thus destroyed its essentially aristocratic character; and a theoretic modification in the same direction was made describing them as the servants instead of the rulers of the community. The relations between believers and unbelievers, or misbelievers, have varied considerably, but the duty of conversion brought the two into intimate social relations, and the customary prohibition of community in marriage and at table is completely removed.

From the doctrine of the complete equality of all men arose the conception of a universal system of ethics, which should be applicable to all Christians; that is to say, potentially, and at last, to the whole world. The duty of all men, whatever their race or their social position, was one, and the final end by which that duty was to be directed was situated not in this world but in another. In this way all national ends were superseded; and antiquity knew no higher. The Roman defined the good man as he who is guided 'by legal precedents, and laws and natural right'; and this ideal, which excludes the pursuit of liberty, he imposed on the conquered world, thereby extinguishing its growth. The aim of Athens was to extinguish liberty in

Greece by imposing her own democratic form of polity on all her subject cities. Her failure opened the door to Macedonian conquest, and converted Hellenic into Hellenistic civilization. For Rome and Greece alike the ideal was in this world and patriotic. The Roman, while highly valuing liberty, gave law the first place. The Athenian undervalued law; the ideal of Alexander was to spread a foreign civilization by military force. The period in antiquity which most nearly attains freedom was at Athens between the expulsion of the Peisistratidae and the death of Pericles, while the higher classes retained a power which was preponderant but not exclusive, and the wisest man among them ruled the State for thirty years with a power which might be compared with that of a constitutional king.

Extension of Law

The new conception of universal liberty does not, in practice, destroy the conception of national freedom. On the contrary, as it is not to be realized on earth, it strengthens it. The practical effect is to enlarge the range of national duty by making it apply to national freedom in all countries, and not only within the boundaries which are subject to its own laws and institutions. With complete liberty on earth, whether for itself or for others, except through the medium of freedom, no national conscience can have any concern without provoking certain failure. The last war of England against France was the struggle of the composite idea of freedom against the simple idea of liberty; and of the two the second was certainly not the one which was most in sympathy with the Christian conscience. When a nation's conscience is penetrated by Christian ideals it recognizes that its duty is not exhausted by the defence of its own freedom, but that it extends to, and embraces, the freedom of all other nations, and ensures that growth in other countries which is necessary to the growth of the whole race of man. It is very far from compelling a complete identity of interest between different nations. On the contrary, its sole object is to secure dissimilarity of growth by allowing to each separate nation the power to pursue its own national ideal along its own lines, and under the protection of its own laws and of its national freedom. Its direct antagonist is the lust for universal conquest, the main end of that being the extinction of rival forms of civilization and the substitution of that of the conqueror.

When international freedom is the end, the same thing occurs to the nation as had previously occurred to the individual on the establishment of national freedom. In the same way as an isolated individual can only become a citizen by the sacrifice of a considerable portion of his private liberty, so can a State only become a member of an international federation by the sacrifice of a material portion of its national liberties. Again, a community of nations can only be kept together by having a common end and a common government, with the powers of making laws for the attainment of that end and the means of enforcing them. There is no good reason to fear that the sentiment of patriotism will be weakened by the growth of the wider devotion to international interests. On the contrary, it is likely to be strengthened. If Rome excelled all other ancient nations in the strength of her patriotism, she excelled them equally in the stringency of her domestic relations. The step in the progression from self to family, from family to nation, and from nation to federal State, are all stages in the advance in comprehension of the spirit of altruism. Its vitality in its upper ranges is strictly dependent on its health in the lower ranges of its comprehension. Unless a man is a good son he cannot be a good citizen; and unless he is a patriotic citizen he is of no value to a wider confederation.

Self-devotion in this world must, of course, be defined and regulated by law, and the higher its range the more necessary is the clear definition of its boundaries. In domestic relations law is less necessary. The power of the Roman paterfamilias was despotic, but it was tempered by the domestic affections and by the customs which grew out of them. Such affections do not exist among nations, and within each are very feebly supplied by the tradition of a common origin. The limit beyond which international law may not be carried is the freedom of each State which is a party to it. The submission to law is only justified, at any stage of development, by one and the same consideration ; it is necessary for the protection of the free activity of the people who submit to it, and when a State submits to law its only justification is that so only can it preserve its own independence and continue to prosecute its own ideals. Peace cannot be accepted as an exclusive final end of international legislation. It may be for a time the happy result, but it can only be preserved by a continuous preparation for war. The occupation of peace is commerce, and the rapid decay in the manly virtues, which sets in as soon as the attention is absorbed in commerce, is too patent to be overlooked by any one who is not a commercial bigot. So long as the international league falls short of embracing the whole of the inhabited world, it will, if it neglects warlike preparations, soon fall a victim to any power, even though it be of a much lower grade of civilization, which chooses to pluck the over-ripe fruit. If it should embrace the whole of humanity, a very remote contingency, and be safe from external dangers, civilization would become stagnant and growth would cease. Again, it is only by the maintenance of considerable force that it could guard against disruption through the discontent or the treachery of one or more of its own members. In order to meet the certain dangers of foreign aggression, of internal disruption, of moral decay, and of loss of the freedom of growth which is of all possessions the most valuable, the international federation must make military strength at least as much its concern as peaceful prosperity. On the other hand the mere possession of arms, in sufficient quantities to preserve the peace, will itself be a powerful provocative to war. αὐτὸς γὰρ ἐφέλκεται ἄνδρα σίδηρος. The only remedy is that every citizen should be at the same time a soldier and a civilian, and that, while giving the first place to commerce and the arts of peace, he should be always ready for war.

For military strength one of the most necessary conditions is unity of command, and this, when the federation is composed of free competing nations, is one of the most difficult to realize. It nearly wrecked the cause of Greece in its contest against the Persians, and no incident in the glorious story of Athens is brighter than its acceptance of the lead of Sparta during the campaign which ended at Plataea. No federation can subsist for long without submitting, when war demands it, and perhaps always, to the military hegemony of one of its component States. England, during the late war, followed the example of Athens in placing her armies under the command of a French marshal; and that is not the least noble of her services to civilization. For its external relations every federation must have a common end, and must submit to the hegemony of one of its own members. And that common end must be the freedom of all, and the enjoyment by each of its own law, except in such special points in which the preservation of the whole demands the sacrifice of a part.

The problem of reconciling the conflicting interests of various nations in such a manner as to leave unhurt the vital interests of all is one of extreme difficulty, far more complicated than the alternative of imposing the civilization of a conqueror on a universal empire. The latter was the solution adopted by the Jews in their dream of a Messianic Kingdom, where the whole world was to be governed by the law of Moses (that is to say, of God), with the chosen people as its ministers. It has been the aim of all world conquests, before and since. The aim of

Alexander was to universalize the culture of Hellas; of the Roman Republic, the peace and law of Rome; of Napoleon, the perfect equality and fraternity of France; of the German Emperor, the peculiar form of German civilization. None of these is compatible with the spirit of Christianity, which has for its final end a perfect equality in heaven, and for its purpose on earth a continual growth which has no end, and which can only be secured by obedience to the law of morality. The growth, dependent on morality, demands the maintenance of a conflict between various ideals. The attempt to maintain them on earth is in consonance with Christian morality: the attempt to destroy them by merging all in one is directly opposed to that, and its success would put an end to further growth.

I had written more on this subject; but all such speculations are in the nature of prophecy in a region where we are wholly blind; and I stop at this point. So blind are we that it is not in our power to single out the special points in our present civilization which are likely to exercise the greatest influence for good or for evil on our future. The discovery of radium, the new art of flying, the political and military awaking of the yellow races are all modifications in our environment, the nature and extent of whose action it is impossible for the best judge to calculate—the teaching of history may possibly be falsified by the abolition of war ; whole races, and those who lead the world to-day, may be brought under the yoke of slavery ; the human race itself may be extinguished, for even religion does not guarantee its perpetuity, and philosophy is confined to the past and present. We must be contented with the remark that it seems certain that our civilization has arrived at a stage when some such step as international federation must be taken; and this is demanded in the interest not of peace but of freedom, and eventually of bare life. Unless law is extended so as to embrace leagues of nations, the freedom of all may be extinguished under a universal empire which would be as much worse than that of Rome as the growth of evil increases with the lapse of time. Civilization would fall a prey to luxury at one end of the social scale and slavery at the other, and there would be no strength left. It would crumble to pieces at the touch of the first virile barbarian who had retained the taste for war ; or, if none such were left, it would fall a prey to worse evils before which war itself would be welcomed as a blessing. There is no war, and no law, when slavery is perfect. The need of international law is only an illustration of the universal principle of the progression of opposites, which demands that every extension of liberty must be gained by a corresponding extension of law.

Freedom—Particular and Universal

It has been asserted that an effete civilization has reason to be grateful when it is conquered by another which is living and in process of further growth. This is plausible, but of doubtful truth. Freedom, or the laws and institutions which are favourable to growth, is a plant which will only flourish on its native soil: when transferred to another it withers and dies. The freedom of America had all the earlier stages of its growth in England, among the same people as those who now enjoy it. When transplanted to America it brought no advantage to the Red Indians, nor is it likely that it should bring any advantage to the peoples of Central Europe if retransplanted there. To them it is an alien form of freedom and, as such, they may reject it. Athens, for the same reason, was hated by the whole of the rest of Greece, and by her own philosophers. It was not the decay of religion that brought her glorious civilization to the dust. Religion, at the period when her decay set in, had lost none of its strength, and was itself in part responsible for her downfall. But we must remember that the religion of the Greek was not the religion of the Christian, and had an opposed ideal. It placed its end in this world, and encouraged aggression and conquest. To the Christian it was the worship of devils, and its loss of power was not to be deplored.

Athens failed through her religion and not in spite of it. Her religion was a State institution and devoted to her own interests to the exclusion of all others. Its utmost range was Panhellenic, and how little she was influenced by that may be seen in all her inter-hellenic history, and especially in the debate at Melos. In her dealings with barbarians she was bound by no law, either express or of moral feeling. It is worth while to remark that, with a level of genius in all other branches which was higher than has been seen in any other State, before or since, she had no general of the first class, whereas her leading enemy, who was otherwise undistinguished, had many. The explanation must be found in her polity. It could not tolerate military excellence. Her one great general was Alkibiades, and to him she twice gave the command, and as often made it impossible for him to retain it. In a sense she may have been right. His victory might have meant the downfall of the democracy. But she had to choose between that and the downfall of the State, and she sacrificed independence to party. Her democracy made military eminence dangerous and impossible. The principle of political equality was given an undue prominence over the principle of merit.

The objection that freedom must be a natural growth tells with equal force against the introduction of English political forms in India. Institutions, whatever they may be, only serve to protect life and growth, and can no more produce them than the soil, however rich, can produce the plant. The institutions are the soil, but freedom is in the spirit and can only be communicated by the spirit. The reproductions of free institutions on an alien soil have no greater value than imitations of Greek architecture or German music. They are lifeless. What restored life to the effete civilizations of the ancient world was the addition of the Christian leaven in the dough of pagan morality. And the leaven that worked the change was the transfer to the end of human action from this world to another. It was this transfer, and this only, that transcended national ideals and made possible the conception of perfect liberty, as an ideal to be striven for, though not to be obtained except by the obedience to law on earth.

A bare collection of moral commandments, issued by a Divine authority, and, by the nature of their origin, debarred from criticism, has no room for comparative ethical values. The man who was guilty of an act of disobedience, in however small a particular, was guilty of the whole law. And this is equally true of all disobedience to the voice of the conscience when reduced to universal maxims, even if they do not claim a Divine origin and a Divine sanction. Kant's test of universality is admitted to be one of the weakest points in his philosophy, and it is enforced by an illustration which is clearly valid to Kant himself but unacceptable to the great majority of mankind. If all the laws of morality were universal we should at once put an end to growth; but the object of morality is to promote growth. The only universal element in morality is Justice, and that is not itself a law but the form in which all its laws must run. The only test which can be applied to morality in order to ascertain the relative value of two conflicting moral commands must be teleological, or with regard to the relative effect on growth.

Our statement involves the assumptions, first of the existence of growth, and secondly that growth is the end of all ethical inquiry, law being the means or necessary conditions of growth and valuable only by reflection, or when it serves its end of promoting growth.

Of what is meant by growth I am no more able to give a philosophical explanation than I can of life. When first I commenced my inquiries I used, for the same concept, the word evolution; but, though that word may very well be applied to the physical development of any living thing, whether plant or animal, from the union of a pair of opposites, under the law of uniform sequence, the growth of an individual or of a race through morality and free will, which is the subject of ethics, demands a distinctive term. The province of the first is in the past; of the second, in the future.

If we require a practical example of what is meant by growth, we need only compare the histories for the last three thousand years of Benares and Westminster. In the first of these, up to the time of the introduction of the British rule, no perceptible change could be observed; at the beginning it had attained a high pitch of civilization, and it maintained the same position at the end. At Westminster, during the same interval, there might be observed a slow progress of growth, through many vicissitudes, from conditions of savagery to a state of civilization much higher than that of Benares. How are we to gauge growth? Perhaps by increase of complexity. But that, though possibly a test of growth, is no test of the power to survive; nor is it a sign of increased hedonistic attractions. Many other cities have reached a more complex civilization than Benares, and have fallen; and its inhabitants are not less happy, on the whole balance of pleasure and pain, than those of Westminster. Pleasures may increase both in variety and in intensity; and in both respects those of Westminster may go beyond those of Benares; but at Westminster the increase of pleasure is counterbalanced by a parallel increase of pain.

The Emotions

We will now consider the emotional colour, by which each of the opposed principles is distinguished. Life, as we stated at the beginning, is the object of all our desires; law, or the principle which restrains life, is the origin of all we hate and fear. The first excites attraction; the second, repulsion. But in this world, where we can have neither without the other, each takes on the tincture of the other, and, though we still love liberty and hate restraint, we approve of neither by itself, but only of both when combined by Justice: that is to say, of freedom. The feeling of approval with which we regard freedom is calm and temperate, and far less violent than the half-insane passion that is inspired by the hope of earthly liberty; but it lasts longer, because it may be realized, whereas the other must end in defeat and despotism, either foreign or domestic. But we must, in comparing the two great movements by which human growth was affected in antiquity with a similar crisis in modern times, remember that the ideals both of Greek and Roman conquests were in their essence despotic;

whereas those of the French revolution were popular, or the liberty of the masses. The difference illustrates the change in popular ethics which Europe had passed through in the interval. But the ideals of Rousseau, though they may inspire passion, cannot be reconciled either with freedom or with Christianity, nor can they ever enjoy a lasting success. In Rousseau's own conviction a Christian republic was a contradiction in terms.

The passion for liberty is indeed the strongest and most compelling of which human nature is susceptible. Liberty is the conditions for unrestrained action, and the desire for it combines all the attractive power of growth with all the repelling power of restraint. It focusses all the passions that are possible to our nature in a single direction. This gives it a strength far above that of the ethical impulses, which are, all of them, combined in nearly even proportions of liberty and law, with a slight balance in favour of the end or purpose, which is added from without. The man who is under the influence of the passion of liberty is indifferent if not actively hostile to the commands both of the conscience and of the laws, whether of private morality or of the State, which are based on it. To patriotism, the highest of the social virtues, he is quite indifferent. The love of liberty dissolves society. It is universal, and implies the love of all mankind. It creates a disposition or temper that is habitually loving, and in that point agrees with Christianity. It differs from Christianity in its bitter enmity to the Church, which is the divinely appointed guardian of law.

Whether the liberty, when it is set up as the sole end of action, is placed in this world or in another, in both cases it destroys all the authority of the moral law and all respect for the conscience; but, in the first case, it does this by falling below it; in the second by rising above it. When the destruction of the moral restraints is placed in this world it means the destruction of all the institutions which are based upon them, and a restoration on earth of the conditions of savagery. It condemns and undoes the whole work of evolution. Logically, it would reduce men to far below the condition of animals, for all growth, however lowly, is dependent on law. Practically, it destroys the particular type of civilization on which the disease has fixed itself, and impels it to contaminate its neighbours with the same disease. Whether there can be any return to life depends on the vitality which remains in the ruins of the institutions it has overthrown. No new life can be imported from without, and if the overthrow has been complete the nation must cease to exist. The effect on the individual of the abolition of law varies with his character, but in none will it be good. The best will devote themselves as missionaries to the spread of their deadly error: for the lower minds it will release the impulses to lust, and cruelty, and avarice, and murder. Of all the enemies to growth it is the worst, and its only value is to clear away a civilization which for other causes has become hopelessly corrupt, and to leave the ground bare for new seed. In a country which, like our own, is already in the possession of freedom, it can do nothing but mischief, and we rightly regard it with the same eyes as we do despotism, as an enemy against which we must put forth our full strength.

When the ideal of liberty is placed not in this world but in another and higher state of existence, its effects are exactly opposite. It fixes the mind on an object which is above all that can be attained in human society, and compels its professor to renounce all earthly aims, whether they be good or bad, as unworthy of its high calling. It dispenses with the help of the conscience and the use of its laws, because their aim is growth in this world, and the whole aim of life, as thus conceived, is external to this world. It is on these grounds that the monk, and the hermit, and the ascetic were, in the Middle Ages, accounted as the true type of a Christian. Such men, if they lived in true conformity with their professed principles, could never be numerous. Worldly society, if they were many, would necessarily cease to exist. But they served as an example to men who remained in the world and who still kept an interest in its strife. For the great majority it was incumbent to fix their minds on a higher world; to adopt the same ideal of perfect liberty in that, and of perfect unselfishness in this, subject only to such conditions as were imposed by the maintenance of life in this world. And the necessary condition of survival is, as we have seen, law. The complete control of the conscience is thus restored for all whose business is in this world, subject to such a modification of direction as will bring it as near as possible in conformity with the heavenly ideal. The Christian mind must, even when the ideal is earthly, always be raised above his present circumstances, and bent on attaining no fixed position (for that is ordained for him in another world) but an increasingly higher level in this. His aim will be to gain as much liberty as is allowed by law, and he will exchange the end of liberty for that of freedom. An ideal which is far above this world produces humility in the worshipper, the more as he rises higher and is more keenly conscious of his own deficiencies: an earthly ideal inspires pride, which increases as the ideal appears to be approached: and a low esteem of one's personal value is favourable to self-sacrifice.

This is far the most comprehensive revolution in

ethical thought that the world has ever witnessed. A recent writer (Mr. B. Kidd) has remarked that before the Christian era the mind of man was turned to the past; and that since then it has been turned to the future. This, on the whole, is a correct generalization, though the revolution is far from having been completed. The interest of Greek philosophy was exclusively in the past, as is that of their modern followers. Its object has been centred in the discovery of a first cause, out of which the whole multiplicity of phenomena has been generated; and the first cause it named reality. The leading interest of the Christian has been transferred from the first cause, or origin, to the final end, or purpose, of all existing things. Finding no single final end in nature, he places it in the mind of God. The first cause must be in the same order with the purpose; and the whole world becomes a creation, with a Divine author and a Divine purpose. Reality is not to be found in this world, but beyond it, in the mind of God.

Greek thought, however, still survives in the form of science and metaphysics. Science is a function of life, and its own value is determined by its effect on life and growth. It has no independent value, but borrows one from the practical effects of its application to life. When it conduces to decay and destruction, as it must when it is employed in a bad cause, it is itself bad; when in a good cause, it is good. It is, in fact, on the same line with force, which is the sign and the invariable concomitant of upward evolution, but is not the final end, because it may be employed in either way, either for the purpose of decay, or for further evolution. In itself science has no relative values, no room for free will, no morality. The Zeus of the Stoic was identified with ἡ πεπρωμένη, or the iron rule of a transcendent scientific law, with which it was useless to contend, and towards which the only proper attitude was one of complete submission. This may appear to be identical with the submission of a Christian to his God; but in effect they are contradictory. The Fate of the Stoic was neither good nor bad; it had neither love nor any other passion, and inspired none in its worshippers. The God of the Christian was a transcendental Person, of perfect goodness and love, and claiming the same class of feelings from his worshippers. All the gods of the pagans, at their best, were personifications of natural law: it was our Lord who first told us that He was Life and Love; and St. Paul that law is the origin of sin, and as such must be rejected. Law is learned by an investigation into the past; the purpose lies necessarily in the future. Science has no place for a God; life cannot exist without one.

The result of giving liberty the precedence over law in the natural world, and regarding the first as the end and the second as the means, will be to put all the various passions which are connected with liberty in the same place, when they are compared with the passions which are connected with law. Love and hate are the most universal of these. Liberty is the object of universal love, and love is the passion which is its characteristic. Law is the object of universal hatred, and hatred is its characteristic passion. But a just law, that is, one that is so ordered as to preserve liberty, is necessary to life, and, though we do not love even a just law, we respect it; it commands our awe. In the same way we no longer love liberty when it is released from law and becomes licence. We then despise it; it is the object of our disgust and our contempt.

The Kingdom of Heaven and the Church on Earth

As our highest ideal is the perfect representation of our final end, our end is in the future; we are debarred from deriving it from a study of the past, because the only thing in the future of which we can be reasonably certain is that, in all features of importance, it will be completely different from the past. If an ape were to set up his ideal on the basis of his own past experience, it would certainly not culminate in a Christian saint. Our growth on the whole has been steadily upward, and if Plato and Helen of Troy be taken as the highest point we have yet reached, they were not constructed from a study of the ages which preceded them, nor will they serve us as ideals for our own future. Nor can they be transformed into ideals by being purged of their faults. A study of the past shows that defects are on the whole race inseparable from merits, and that a supposed perfection, at any stage, is equivalent to extinction. The only reasonable ideal which can serve man's purposes on earth must be supernatural or Divine. It must have neither beauty nor strength; and it must be sinless or above the law. The moral law gives neither end nor direction, but only bare imperatives. When guided in the direction of liberty in another world it gives the preference to those moral impulses within this world which are appropriate to liberty, over those which are appropriate to law. In the conflict between love and jealousy it gives a decided preference to love; it sets co-operation higher than competition, and approves of competition only in those cases where it serves the end of co-operation. Patriotism is the highest form of competition because it involves the greatest degree of individual self-sacrifice. Still, the self-sacrifice is not the end. It is merely the means to national self-assertion, and the end prescribes the character of the moral impulses which are to take the lead. Love is still highly valued, but it must be used in the service of national jealousy. When, however, love takes the lead, our horizon is widened. Our patriotism is as much needed as ever, and we must still be no less jealous of our neighbours than we were, but our end is a universal love, and our jealousy is justified only as a means for the protection of the freedom of others. When that is threatened we must fight, as indeed we must fight for our own freedom. Like the unjust steward, we must take such measures as are needed for the preservation of our own lives, and, far from being blamed, we shall be received into eternal mansions. Moreover, when love is the leading impulse, we can, while retaining our patriotism unaffected, rise above it, and take thought for the interests of the whole race. Without faith in another world our only guide is science; our only God is force; and the philosophy of Clausewitz is irrefutable. The final end of that is victory for the nation; the ultimate result is degradation and ruin for the race. With faith in another world, the final end on this world is freedom, or life, for the whole human race, and victory is the means to that; and with that end in view, patriotism, with all the force which its maintenance dictates, is justified. Self-sacrifice is no longer the means to competition, but the means to a wider co-operation.

In short, the ethical inquirer, who refuses to be contented with a dualist conception of life but presses on to unity, is compelled to accept the religious doctrine of immortality, and to believe that the soul of the individual (however that may be defined) passes from life in this world to life in a world beyond it. Of the state of the soul before birth he knows nothing, and it is of no importance to him that he should. Philosophy can no more deal with the reality of the soul than it can with the idea of God; both, so far as they can be dealt with by the human reason, are the subjects of Theology, or the knowledge that is based on religious faith.

The resolution which is given by Christianity to this dualism of liberty and law is that there is another life for the soul, subsequent to this life, in which the soul will enjoy perfect liberty and be unrestrained by law. This means that the conscience will cease to exist; its place will be taken by the love of God, and the soul will be filled with His glory and His joy. Admission to this state, which is called the kingdom of God in heaven, is open to men on earth, but only on the condition that they divest themselves of all earthly interests.

This condition is not only theoretical, but a clear practical necessity; for the introduction of earthly interests must necessarily bring with it the control of the conscience, and the control, so far, of the perfect liberty of the kingdom of God in heaven. The rejection of the guidance of the conscience, and the substitution of liberty in another world, raises a man above either good or evil, and its attainment depends not on works but on faith only. The adoption of liberty in this world, and the rejection of the value of the conscience, is sheer licence and immorality. The destruction of law is at the same time the destruction of life, and any undue check on the growth of law tends in the same direction.

For those who retain their position in this world and are still engaged by its cares and its interests, the empire of the conscience is necessary to the preservation of the life of themselves and of their posterity. But the mass of its precepts will receive a new direction. Its final end will be transferred from this world to another and a better, in which the constraints of the conscience, and with them all that is evil, will be removed. There, beyond the world of experience, there will be neither growth to promote nor decay to avoid: here, there must always be both, and, so long as there is either, there is still the necessity of law. When conscience is eliminated, change and distinctions disappear. But the soul itself remains, and, being without a moral clothing, must either be perfectly good or perfectly bad. It must either be above or below morality. The aim of action in this world is the attainment in another world of perfect liberty and the avoidance of perfect slavery. So long as he remains in this world a man can have neither, but he puts liberty before him as his end, and retains law only so far as it is required as a means for the preservation and promotion of liberty in life. This is also the proper end of conscience. The aim of the kingdom on earth, as well as of morality, is freedom and not liberty. Its reward, but not its aim, is pure liberty in another world. And this, though philosophy, being wholly concerned with actions and their motives, cannot directly take account of it, is promised by religion. For men who remain in this world a perfect life in the next is promised, as a reward for acts in this which are in accordance with the law of God, and with the commands of a rightly directed conscience. If left to itself philosophy must be dualist and have no single final end, and religion, if based on philosophy, Manichee. The Christian religion rejects philosophy; it refuses its sanction to all moral valuations; and it declares an end beyond the world, which is gained not by good works but by a heaven-sent faith. It further provides, for our obedience in the conduct of worldly affairs, a Church, which shall guide our steps, through good works, in the direction of no earthly end, but of the heavenly end, which is perfect liberty.

LIBERTY

THE KINGDOM OF HEAVEN

LIBERTY

THE KINGDOM OF HEAVEN

The Double Nature of Our Lord

THE central dogma in Christianity, from which all the various beliefs radiate, is a unity of opposites—the human and the divine—in one person. In the words of Pascal (*Pensées*, xxiv. 12), 'La foi embrasse plusieurs vérités qui semblent se contredire. La source en est l'union de deux natures en Jésus-Christ.' And again (in the same article), 'Tous hérétiques errent d'autant plus dangereusement qu'ils suivent chacun une vérité. Leur faute n'est pas de suivre une fausseté, mais de ne pas suivre une autre vérité.' Nearly all the heresies which have distracted the Church, and endangered the accomplishment of its mission on earth, have proceeded from the exclusive insistence on one of the elements in the double nature and the denial or neglect of the other. If, with the Arians, we had eliminated the Divine element, our faith would not differ in any material respect from that of Islam; if, with the Doketics, the human, it would have been a pantheist philosophy presiding over a popular polytheism. In neither case would our present civilization, or perhaps any advance in civilization, have been realized. Each of the two natures gives rise to a separate and, potentially, independent system of belief: and Christianity, like the Person of its Founder, is a combination of the two systems; of which neither can be omitted without the destruction of the whole fabric. One system corresponds with the Divine nature, and deals with God's kingdom in heaven and in the soul of man; the other, with the human nature, and deals with His kingdom on earth and in the affairs of daily life. The basis of Christian ethics is the double will: the Divine will, which is above the law; and the human will, which is perfect obedience.

History

Both systems find their germs in the most ancient traditions of the Hebrews. The doctrine of the heavenly kingdom is derived, with direct connexion, from the story of the creation, first of the world and secondly of man; and with the degeneration of both through the disobedience of man. The kingdom on earth is derived from the promise to Abraham of universal dominion on earth. The two are sharply contrasted in the first pair of Beatitudes (Vulgate arrangement): 'Blessed are the poor in spirit, for theirs is the kingdom of heaven: blessed are the meek, for they shall inherit the earth.' The former places salvation in faith, the latter in works; in one the Redeemer is the crucified Lord, who died and was buried, and rose again and ascended into heaven: in the other He is the living Bridegroom of the Church on earth.

Not only are the origins from distinct elements within the same tradition, but the descent of each has been by a distinct line and through separate representatives. The tradition of the heavenly kingdom has had for its ideal a perfect liberty, and for its representatives the prophets. The earthly kingdom is based on the law; and the minister and guardian of the law has been the priest. The agencies, and their respective doctrines, have been not only distinct but actively antagonistic, and the Jewish priests are well known as having been the murderers of the prophets. In Christianity the lines have been preserved and combined in the double nature. Our Lord, on his Divine side, is the creative Word beyond time; on his human side, our perpetual High Priest. In the Western Church before the Reformation the latter was represented by the priests and the Papal government; the former by the monks, so long as they obeyed their original mission. The legend which connects the origin of the monks with Mount Carmel embalms an important spiritual truth.

Contrast between the Two Kingdoms

From our point of view, what is important in a doctrine is not its origin, nor its history, but its effects on human conduct, and it is in this respect that the tendencies which distinguish the two doctrines, whose combination makes up the full body of Christianity, are most plainly and radically opposed. The tendency of the doctrine of the heavenly kingdom is destructive: it has no positive law and no morality; in politics it is nihilist. The tendency of the earthly kingdom, on the contrary, is constructive and conservative; it respects wealth, and is the main bulwark of morality. The first is the religion of the poor, the second, of the rich; but neither can stand alone; or by itself, or without the other, is Christianity. Tolstoy, in his nihilist novel *Resurrection*, quotes at length the greater part of the Sermon on the Mount, but he makes no pretence to be a Christian, and is hostile to the religion as a whole, rejecting and hating the Church. On the other hand, an excessive attention to the doctrine of salvation by works at one time brought the Church to the verge of destruction, and gave rise to practices and principles of action which must very soon have destroyed civilization. The combination of the two opposites in a single individual creed is Christianity. It has been the parent of our present civilization, and its preservation is essential to the maintenance and the further advance of our civilization in the future.

Jewish Law categorical, but no Autonomy

Before proceeding to more detailed accounts of each of these conflicting bodies of doctrine separately, it will be as well to state quite definitely that in no part of the Jewish system is there the faintest trace of an attempt to supply a philosophical or metaphysical basis to its theory of human conduct. The sole guide to right action is the voice of God, whether expressed in the written law or in tradition. The sole virtue is obedience to that; the sole offence, disobedience. There may be many desirable results from obedience. For example—length of days is promised, as a reward, to him who honours his parents; but dishonour is punished as a sin, not because the reward is missed, but because the commandment is disobeyed—all things must be done for the glory of God, and for no other reason. All inquiry into the results of action is wholly irrelevant to the question as to whether it is to be classed as good or evil. A virtuous action is one that is done from no earthly consideration: neither from care, nor fear, nor utility, nor desire of pleasure, nor from sense of honour; but merely for the glory of God; 'in my name'. The reward promised to the Jews is that they shall be 'above all nations in praise and in name and in honour; and a holy people' (Deut. xxvi. 17–19). But this is to be gained by obedience to the voice of God, whatever it may command. The future, and the whole purpose of God, is unfathomable.

The practical resemblance between this and Kant's theory of the categorical imperative is obvious. Both exclude all reference to consequences. They contradict all forms of Utility, or Eudemonism, and all striving after any human ideal, even of the very highest, as a universal end of action. But the difference is equally important. The law of the Jews was external; it was promulgated in writing or by word, by priest or by prophet, for the guidance of an obedient people. The moral command of Kant is given to each individual by his own conscience. Moral laws are, no doubt, generalized from the special commands of the conscience, but they have no universal authority, and where a man's conscience contradicts them his duty is to obey that and not the laws. Each individual is in the strictest sense autonomous.

We may now proceed to a nearer consideration of the doctrine of salvation by faith and not by works: that is, the doctrine of the heavenly kingdom.

Difference in kind between God and man

Its history begins with the creation of the world out of nothing, and of man out of the dust. This doctrine provides an answer to all philosophic theories of actual or eventual identity of the human and the Divine. The difference between the Creator and the creation is not one of degree but of kind. The creation we know; of the Creator it is impossible that we should know anything except what He is pleased to reveal to us. Our inquiries into nature make us acquainted with certain laws of great generality. Uniform sequence, continual change, change in a fixed direction, an alternative direction, in advance or in retreat, are all of them principles of movement which we think we observe, and strive to define; but of the original cause and the final destination of ourselves, and of the medium in which we live, we have no rational idea, and except in revelation no trustworthy basis for forming one.

The doctrine of the creation of the world out of nothing is a vital element in the Christian conception of life. According to that, the world in which we live is full of corruption, and under the dominion of death; and it must so continue until it is replaced by the kingdom of heaven, in which corruption will put on incorruption, and there will be no death. But end and beginning are terms of which each implicates the other. ταῦτα ἀλλήλοις ἀκολουθεῖ, καὶ τό τε ἀγένητον ἄφθαρτον καὶ τὸ ἄφθαρτον ἀγένητον... εἰ γενητόν τι, φθαρτόν ἀνάγκη.[1] Death and birth are correlatives, and so, equally, are growth and decay, and all forms of instability. Those are the forms of life on earth. The gift of salvation is to substitute for them an eternal life in heaven, where there is no change and the principles are immutable.

The effect of this doctrine is to establish a complete distinction in kind, and not merely in degree, between the Creator and the creature. A complete distinction is one which excludes from one object all the attributes of the other, and of this kind is the distinction between God and man. The worst man agrees with the best in being human; so, equally, does the second best man. All distinctions between men are in degree, not in kind. Our Lord Himself in His human character, though perfect man, disclaims the attribution of goodness; and He assigns His truths to revelation from the Divinity. It follows that no substantial communication between the Divine and the natural is even conceivable.

---

[1] Quoted by Schopenhauer, *Willen in der Natur*, p. 142, from Aristotle, *de Caelo*, i. 12. Aristotle copied it from the Eleatics.

There are no points of contact, and all pantheistic interpretations of life are contradicted. The attempt to deduce from the creation the attributes of the Creator is idolatry and the parent of uncleanness. It has been handed down to us from the Greeks; to the Jews it was always abhorrent. The communication, by grace, to humanity of some of the Divine attributes is widely different from its endowment with the whole or of any part of the Divine nature. It may amount to an imitation, but never to identity. The soul of man may be like God, eternal, but through all eternity it must remain distinct, and of a different order from Him. Christian mysticism is a contradiction in terms. The concept of the absorption of the soul in God is not Christian but pantheist. Revelation, through possession by the Holy Spirit, implies no absorption of the human personality. The distinction of the third Person in the Trinity definitely precludes *identification* with the substance. St. Paul discriminates between commands which are issued by the indwelling Spirit of Christ and his own personal opinions; and his inspiration is clearly identical in kind with that of all the disciples on the day of Pentecost, of the household of Cornelius, and indeed of the whole body of believers. It is only distance in point of time, and a want of acquaintance with that class of phenomena, that leads men to seek an explanation in Hellenic pantheism. Even the beatific vision differs from absorption in preserving the distinction of persons. In this lies the main significance of the resurrection of the body.

Fall of Man through Disobedience

The next step in the history is the fall of man through disobedience to a Divine command. Originally man shared with the animal creation a life of ignorant happiness. This he lost, and acquired, instead, the knowledge of good and evil. As a punishment for his disobedience, and not as a result of the knowledge, he and the earth are cursed, and his life is to be full of labour and sorrow. These conditions, however, are not to be eternal; a final deliverance is promised to the seed of the woman. From this tradition is developed the doctrine of our redemption by a Divine mediator.

As a consequence of the curse, the whole creation now lies under the power of death and the prince of darkness. But the curse can only be released by the same power from which it originally proceeded. For this purpose it was necessary that the power of God should be united with the seed of the woman, to whom the victory over evil is promised. We may again quote Pascal (*Pensées*, xxii. 9, 10): 'Sans Jésus-Christ, il faut que l'homme soit dans le vice et dans la misère; avec Jésus-Christ l'homme

MAN FELL THROUGH DISOBEDIENCE 179

est exempt de vice et de misère. En lui est toute notre vertu, et toute notre félicité. Hors de lui, il n'y a que vice, misère, erreurs, ténèbres, mort, désespoir. Sans Jésus-Christ le monde ne subsisterait pas : car il faudrait, ou qu'il fût détruit, ou qu'il fût comme un enfer.' The equivalent to this in terms of Ethics would be this : without the influence of Christianity the whole world would degenerate, and the animal impulses prevail over the higher and more lately developed attributes of humanity.

Restoration and Perfect Liberty

The new creation is not an improvement on the old, but a new state of things; a καινὴ κτίσις, the difference, like the difference between God and man, is complete; the old creation is wholly bad, the new, wholly good; there is no point of contact, and no causal connexion. The natural man can do nothing that is good; even if he could, it would give him no title to citizenship in a world which differed in all ways from his own. The concept of merit disappears, and the new citizenship is a free gift, conditioned only by faith in its existence on the part of the devotee and a fervent desire for its attainment. Even to desire it is a grace, and can never be claimed as a right. In its essence, it is a new temper, or disposition, which is wholly released from law. It is no longer freedom, but a complete liberty. This is the feature which accounts for the extreme antipathy aroused by early Christianity in pagan society. The Jews, by rejecting idols, were counted as atheists; the Christians went further, and in rejecting law, as well as images, make a third race, the lowest in the scale of human beings. Nothing, indeed, could be more natural in cultivated minds, whose end of action was happiness in this life, than the belief that the rejection of the moral law would lead to degradation and unhappiness. Such a rejection would in fact have been not so much degrading as impossible, had it stood alone as the whole religion, and not been supplemented by the doctrine and institutions of God's kingdom on earth.

A perfect liberty is to be realized only by a complete renunciation of human interests. All action in this world is strife, and the highest provokes the strongest opposition. It is no exaggeration to assert that the merit of an action in the right direction may be measured by its difficulty. The ideal of liberty can only be obtained under conditions of isolation, where each man lives for and by himself. The perfect Christian from this point of view is the monk; and the best form of monk, the anchorite of the desert. This gives full opportunity for the love of God, but none whatever for love of your neighbour; and it is remarkable how scarce and lukewarm are the references to public service and the help of others, which occur in books of Christian devotion such as the *Imitatio Christi*. The imitation is indeed imperfect, and of one side only of the compound character of Christ. No life is more widely removed from that of our Lord than that of the monk or the anchorite.

To a man who holds this form of Christianity only, and rejects the earthly kingdom of the Church, not only is action of all kinds immaterial as a means for the attainment of the heavenly kingdom, but it remains equally valueless after that kingdom has been attained. Sin neither debars entry, nor, after entry, entails loss. If he is in a state of grace, good actions are of no advantage and sinful actions do no harm; even religious observances, such as public worship and the celebration of the sacred mysteries, are irrelevant, and had better be discontinued. Each man is king and bishop over himself, and has no duty but to follow his own will. The Moravian leader, Count Zinzendorf, tells John Wesley: 'Abnegationem omnem respuimus, conculcamus. Facimus, credentes, omne quod volumus, et nihil extra. Mortificationem omnem ridemus.'[1] Liberty, even in this life, is perfect. There is no law.

[1] J. Wesley's *Journal* (Everyman's Library), vol. i, p. 326.

A lively description of the Beghards, a sect which represented the same principle in Flanders and North Germany in the thirteenth and fourteenth centuries, is given by their contemporary John Tauler :

> They think they are free from sin, and united to God without any means whatever, and that they have got above all subjection to the Holy Church, and above the commandments of God, and above all works of virtue; for they think this emptiness so noble a thing that it may not be hindered by ought else. . . . They deem that if they work, it hindereth the work of God. . . . They would fain be free from all those things wherewith the Holy Church is concerned ; and they say openly that a man, so long as he strives after virtue, is still imperfect. . . . They believe they may do freely, and without sin, whatever nature desireth—there is no law nor commandment for them, and therefore they follow all the lusts of the flesh, &c.

The whole passage is worth reading. The teaching of the Lollards in England, and of many sects in the south of France, was largely imbued with the same spirit. It is the spirit which attempts to realize universally on earth the liberty of the kingdom of God in heaven, and rejects the restraints which are imposed by the Church of God on earth. It is the destruction of religion ; in the

---

[1] Tauler's *Life and Sermons* (Winkworth), p. 159, note.

same way as the social principles of Rousseau are destructive of civilization.

The Kingdom of Heaven and Free Will

The pursuit of perfect liberty in this life is in practice antinomian. And its elevation to the highest place among the principles of conduct is the mark which mainly distinguishes Christianity from Judaism. To the Jew the law was all in all. The Christian worship was neither here nor in Jerusalem, but in truth and in spirit. Even in Christianity, however, the law though superseded was not abrogated. It must remain as long as heaven and earth endure. But, though heaven and earth must pass away, the message of Christ, that is, life eternal and the kingdom of heaven, shall not pass away. The kingdom of heaven is above, and must survive the law. What then is life eternal when the earth and the heavens have passed away? It is the timeless contemplation by the individual soul of the love and glory of God. Of any further positive content the mind can form no conception.

That life involves a complete release from the moral law, and where there is no moral law there is no longer any room for the concept of free will. Free will, or the power to refuse obedience, is the concept which distinguishes moral law from natural system.

As Dante says, 'alone of all created things man is invested with it', and for that reason it is valued more highly than any other gift of God, because man values most of all things his supreme position in the order of creation. It is valued moreover as being the only means through which he can retain that position and further exalt it. The moral law is the sole condition to that; obedience to the moral law is the sole standard of merit; and there is no merit where there is no free will. Again, though constituting the highest of earthly goods, it is confined to this world, and does not reach beyond it. Animals must conform with natural law or die, and they rise and fall in the scale of evolution, like the waves of the sea, because they have no free will and no conscience to guide it. In heaven, evolution has ceased, and there is no place for obedience where the soul at last has no intentions but such as are completely in conformity with the will of God. The leading distinction between the kingdom on earth and the kingdom in heaven is that the former exalts to the highest pitch of value the concept of free will; the latter, by denying the possibility of disobedience, transcends it.

In the pure doctrine of the kingdom of heaven, that is, of salvation by faith, there is no place in any of its stages for the conception of a free will. Perfect liberty admits of no control, and casts forth freedom. But where there is no free will there is neither merit nor responsibility, and no basis for morality. When therefore the doctrine of the kingdom of heaven takes its place in the morality of the Church it necessarily accepts the universal formula of freedom of the will. It will be remembered that in that position its function is to oppose the law, but it opposes rather as a friend than as an enemy; for neither law nor liberty can exist on earth unless each is controlled by the other. The doctrine of the Church then strongly asserts the freedom of the will and the personal responsibility of every man for his actions. Freedom of the will, which has no place in the kingdom of heaven, takes the first place in the moral postulates of the kingdom on earth. In the world of creation a belief in the freedom of the will is strained to the utmost limit of its powers, to maintain its own place above a belief in law in the pair of opposites which, together, constitute freedom.

The creation of man is described in Genesis as a double process. First God formed his body out of the dust of the ground, then He breathed into his nostrils the breath of life, and he became a living soul. The dust of the ground is the whole of evolving nature, what the Hindu calls the Sansar, which endures for a time, and, with all its contents, Gods and men included, comes to an end; only to start again on another round in time. The breath of life, which makes man a living soul, and thereby distinguishes him from the rest of creation, is the second self of consciousness which sits above the created part of man as a spectator of his conduct. It gives man a free choice of action and the liberty to obey or to disobey the laws of morality. It thus gives rise to the notions of responsibility and personal merit, and to the rules of morality which are founded on those notions. It does not exempt him from the law of nature, but it enables the reason, in science, to modify that law in any direction, and to a degree to which no limits have been discovered. But in the phenomenal world we have neither the prospect of complete liberty nor its promise. *Non nisi parendo imperamus.*

The conception of the reality of the transcendental self is purely Christian. Among the Greeks and the Jews the real self was the form, of which the soul was nothing but a helpless reflection. 'Their souls he sent to Hades: their selves he left a prey to dogs and vultures' and 'the helpless flocks of the dead';[1] and the ghosts which answered the call of the Witch of Endor. The self or body of Hercules was in Heaven, his soul in Hades. The same conception of the transcendental self, as

---

[1] Κάρηνα, 'bare, unqualified number'; as in the phrase κάρηνα βοῶν—'head of cattle'.

reflecting like a mirror the actions of the living self but itself devoid of will or reason or feeling, lies at the basis of the Samkya philosophy in India, which is therefore rightly regarded as materialist. But it is not only materialism, but the whole of Greek thought, and of the modern metaphysics derived from it, which place reality in the world of actual or possible apprehension, that are excluded from reality in the doctrine of salvation by faith. With us the reality of the self transcends phenomena, and is not cognizable by the scientific reason. It survives the annihilation of the world, as supreme, though not alone. The connexion between the spiritual and the natural element is so intimate that it can never be dissolved. There can be no soul without an intellect.

Ethics of the Kingdom of Heaven

The extra-phenomenal will, when it co-operates with, or obeys, the Divine will in an act of the new creation, has for its object a complete emancipation from the burdens of the old creation, and its rules or tendencies will be wholly destructive. It will be, in spirit, Nihilist. Its direction will be opposed to that of the natural will, which it will be its concern to thwart and eventually to eradicate, in order to leave a free space to be occupied by the new creation.

If it is remembered that life on earth is, in fact, nothing else but a means or preparation for the real life of the world to come, the difficulty becomes less formidable. In order to qualify itself for a life of perfect liberty, the human self must divest itself of its qualifications for the world of law. That is to say, man must free himself from all the tendencies and passions which justify constraint and make it necessary. He must become half a man, and no longer a citizen of the world of evolution, before he can reach perfection. It is this tendency which explains the acceptance by Tolstoi, and others like him, of the Sermon on the Mount, and their rejection of the Christianity of the Church.

We may illustrate this from the ethics of the kingdom of heaven. Their leading principle, which indeed sums up the whole rule of conduct, is love: love of God, and love of your neighbour. The two are the same thing, and the meaning is this: the complete self-sacrifice to the commands of God must be inspired by the willing co-operation of every constituent element in a man's nature; by love, and not through fear of punishment, which implies a love of what is forbidden. Love of things of this world is forbidden, and, before all things, that form of love on which the preservation of the race is dependent. In the first ages of the Church many of her most devoted sons willingly rendered

ETHICS OF THE KINGDOM OF HEAVEN 189

themselves incapable of marriage; and the Church, in self-defence, was obliged to exclude such men from the priesthood. Of both stages Origen, the greatest of the early Fathers, was an example. But, though the body which he sacrificed was to be preserved unmaimed, celibacy was still the highest virtue. It filled the cloisters with monks, and was eventually made a necessary qualification for the Roman priesthood. Mutilation was forbidden on the same grounds as suicide. It was an evasion of the contest. Nevertheless, the highest type of Christian remained the monk: his highest aim involved the destruction of humanity.

Professor Harnack expressed surprise at the influence which St. Augustine (*Successor Pauli*) has exercised within the Roman Church. 'That the Church became at one and the same time Caesarian and Augustinian is the most important and marvellous fact in its history.' It was the direct consequence of the union of God and man in the nature of Jesus Christ, and of the combination in his successor on earth of duty to preserve on earth both the kingdom of faith and the kingdom of works. The Church on earth was compelled by its position, which combined the functions both of the prophet and of the priest, not only to maintain tradition, but further to define and where necessary to amplify it. Wherever the interpreting power may be held to reside, whether in the Bishop of Rome as the supreme head, or in the aristocracy of a council, or in the whole body of the faithful, its decisions were dictated by the Holy Spirit, and were superior to reason. The only point which was open to controversy was whether the authority was properly constituted. It might be the supreme Pontiff of modern Rome, or the Council, as at Nicaea, or at times in mediaeval Europe; or the inner light of the Quaker, which illuminates each individual believer.

Celibacy of the Clergy

The effect of the Augustinian principle may be illustrated by a few words on the discipline of celibacy of the clergy.

The Church, both in the West and in the East, was, as has been observed, broken up into two orders, the monks and the regular clergy, after the pattern of the Jewish division of prophet and priest, and the life of the monk was guided by the new spirit of the kingdom of faith, whereas the life of the priest was a continuation of the old Jewish dispensation of law. In the Jewish Church no rule for the celibacy of the priest was known. It was a hereditary order, and all its members were married. Marriage was necessary in order to maintain the

CELIBACY OF THE CLERGY

succession. In the early Church, in the same way, there was no rule of celibacy. St. Peter was married, and so, probably, were all the apostles except St. Paul. But the Christian Church differed from the Jewish in two important respects. In the first place there was no hereditary order to keep up; in the second place it had two separate dispensations to maintain: first the Jewish law, which our Lord declared should remain in force as long as the heavens and the earth endured; and, secondly, the dispensation of the heavenly Kingdom, which was above law.

The Jewish law contained no rule against marriage, and our Lord commends it as the highest of all earthly relations, making the tie much stricter than it had been, and in no ways restricting it to the laity. For the Christian, as the inheritor of the Jewish law, there was no reason against the marriage of the clergy, and many in its favour. On the other hand, it was incumbent on the clergy to preach the kingdom of heaven; and there our Lord distinctly declares there is no marriage: *neque nubent.* St. Paul, while admitting the legality of marriage, strongly prefers celibacy. In none of these utterances is any distinction drawn between the two orders of laymen and clergy: they are addressed to all alike; and to whichever order a man belonged he was equally free to choose whether he would marry or remain single. After a painful and protracted struggle, the Church finally succeeded in withdrawing this option from the clergy. And here it was no doubt moved by the spirit of St. Paul and St. Augustine, that is, of the kingdom which is above law.

In this way the clergy escaped the reproach of preaching a restraint which they did not themselves practise. They at the same time proved by their own example that obedience neither exceeded human powers nor unfitted a man from taking his place in society. And they incurred no just suspicion of personal pride. To have many wives might be a credit to oneself; to have none was to the glory of God only.

A further result was that it contributed materially to the political stability of the constitution of the Church. We have seen, first, that no government can hope to stand which does not represent merit as well as numbers, and secondly that we have no trustworthy test of merit. In order to maintain the representation of merit which is indispensable, some artificial test must be substituted for the direct one, which it is impossible to apply. Of these artificial tests for the constitution of an aristocracy we may mention four—men may be distinguished either by their wealth, or by their birth, or by office, or by learning. This is not the place for comparing their respective advantages; what concerns us is that the celibacy of the clergy preserved the Church from a hereditary aristocracy and secured an aristocracy of office. It was thus saved from the intolerable burden of a priestly caste, like the tribe of Levi among the Jews or the Brahmans in India. A hereditary priesthood, in its internal relations, would have extinguished the light of the spirit; in its outer, it would have either stopped further progress in civilization or have been itself overthrown by a revolt. The danger of a Levitical caste no longer exists, but in the Middle Ages it was very real. The present Latin Church is based on a pure democracy, guided by an aristocracy, which, not being of birth, must be, in the main, of personal merit; and it has escaped, so far, the risks of an exclusive devotion to priestly interests, as well as those of either ossification, or, at least for the last four centuries, of disruption. It discharges its functions with regularity and success, and it still retains a place for the prophetic as well as for the priestly spirit. In all this the leading cause must be found in the celibacy of its clergy, which raises them, in one important respect, above earthly interests. The esteem with which they are regarded by neighbours, who are often inspired by a theologic hatred, proves that their continence has been strong enough to resist the strain to which it has been exposed. Their enemies expect its failure, would give the utmost publicity to every breach of the rules, and would invent them, if the case were such that there was any prospect that they would be believed.

Self-repression

All the other principles of action in the religion of faith are directly anti-social. Next in importance to celibacy is, perhaps, the total avoidance of conflict and of the self-assertion which leads to it. But conflict is the first condition of advance in civilization. The first movement, and every subsequent step in evolving life, is derived from the active opposition of competing principles, which finally reveal themselves in the conflicting interests of individuals or of nations. This is equally true both of trade and of war; both are essentially competitive, and they are equally opposed to the spirit of the Divine kingdom in heaven. Without earthly love, without commerce, without the exalting self-devotion of war, the spirit of art will find no home. We shall have no great public buildings, or statues, or pictures, or music, or anything that rejoices and elevates the mind of man. A gorgeous ritual, and noble architecture, such as distinguished the Temple at Jerusalem, are not only opposed to

SELF-REPRESSION

the spirit of faith, but their disappearance is plainly foretold. 'Neither in this place, nor in Jerusalem shall ye worship the Father, but in spirit and in truth.'

The doctrine of Faith favours poverty

It is, I think, clear that the doctrine of faith lays down no practical rules for conduct in either private or public life. Its sole injunction is negative. It enjoins an abstinence without reserve. The distinctions of rank and fortunes and intellect, and all that gives one man a precedence over another, or serves as a source of power, are part of the world which will be superseded, and are no advantage, but a positive disqualification for the new kingdom. To Lazarus, in the parable, is ascribed no virtue, to Dives no vice: the sole distinctions are poverty and wealth. It is wealth only and not demerit that keeps the rich man from the kingdom of God: it is extreme poverty, and not virtue, that gains it. All political movement is for the attainment of the goods of this world, and the fleeting goods of this world disqualify their owner for the real and eternal goods of the next.

Christianity has been mainly the religion of the poor. How this came about we may learn from history. The great body of professing Christians has from the first been divided into two sections between the doctrines of salvation by grace and salvation by works. During the centuries while the Church at Rome maintained the Imperial unity of the West, both parties flourished under the same impartial administration. It was only when the governing body gave an undue prominence to the doctrine of works that the adherents of the doctrine of faith cast off their allegiance. Before that time the main home of the doctrine was with the monks or religious orders; of the conflicting doctrine, the secular clergy; and we find that it was the first who asserted the equality of all men; the second who furnished and supported the institutions which kept alive their inequality. We find the same distinction in England, where the Established Church is strongly conservative, and dissent, overwhelmingly liberal. In the days when the Church was undivided, it was the Lollards who kept alive both doctrines of salvation by faith and of political equality; and the secular clergy, their opposites. After the Reformation the distinction has been maintained by the High and Low parties within the Church, and by the opposition between the Established Church and dissent outside it. John Wesley attempted to strengthen the element of the heavenly kingdom within the Church; but, like Luther, he was rejected by the Church he belonged to. Luther's revolt was the signal for the outbreak of the Peasants' War, and though he had no personal sympathy it was a part of the same movement as his.

The doctrine of Works favours the rich

Of the two opposites out of which Christianity is woven, the main or leading doctrine, which distinguishes it from all other religions, and gives it its peculiar direction, is that of the kingdom of heaven; and the function of the earthly kingdom, though it is quite indispensable, is subordinate; that it is to say, to keep alive, in a world of evolution, where the good and evil principles are always in conflict, the senior and governing principle. Hence it is fair to regard as the leading direction in the political influence of the religion that direction which accords with, though it may not be precisely the same as, that of its leading doctrine. On one side Christianity favours the poor, on the other, it supports the princes of the world; it lends its influence impartially to liberty and to authority; and its operation is through two parties within itself, which roughly correspond with the prophet and the priest; but the prophet takes precedence, and throughout the Middle Ages it was the monk who was the type of religious perfection;

the crown and the flower of holiness. The various orders of monks which arose within the Church before the Reformation had for their mission the reaffirmation of the kingdom of heaven and the doctrine of faith, in a Church in which the interests of the kingdom of earth, with its doctrine of works, were daily gaining the mastery. The Jesuit, the chief monastic order that has arisen since the Reformation, has transposed the relative positions of the two aims, and has definitely subordinated the kingdom of heaven to the aims of the kingdom on earth. It transfers the lead and typical representation of the Christian life and spirit from the prophet to the priest, and its main field of labour from the cottage to the palace. Lazarus is postponed to Dives.

The conflict, in fact, extends throughout the whole history of Christianity. It had its roots in Judaism, and is still being waged with a vigour that increases with time. On the one hand, the doctrine of the complete equality of all men induces an opposition to rank and class: a firm conviction of the unreality of all worldly pleasure discredits the pursuit and the possession of the means to attain it; and the belief that the world is governed by the prince of darkness is hostile to the actual government, whatever it may be. All together, they give rise to a strong sympathy with the poor and undistinguished multitudes, irrespective of any comprehension or approval of their aims. On the other hand we have the necessary ecclesiastical organization for the maintenance of morality within the religion itself, and, through that, for the preservation of the place of the religion within the world of evolution. That requires wealth and power for itself, and sympathizes with them in others.

Advantages in this life of a Faith which transcends Morality

Neither religion nor morality gives a reason which is based on the probable consequences in this world of acting or refusing to act in the way which it indicates. Action in both cases is discriminated by obedience or disobedience to a bare command. At this point the resemblance ceases. The command proceeds, in morality, from the inner man; in religion from an external God. The purpose of morality is situated, within this world, in the maintenance of the human race; of religion, in the salvation or the perfection of the individual in a world to come. The sanction of one is remorse, of the second a future life of misery; the rewards, satisfaction in this world or eternal bliss in the next. The external support of morality is the State and the law; of religious virtue, the Church and its ordinances. The life of faith is raised above both State and Church.

Within Christianity the principle which distinguishes the doctrine of faith from the doctrine of works, in the province of private action, lies in their respective attitudes in regard to the conscience and the rules of morality. The rule of faith entirely disregards them. Its aim is perfect liberty, and it soars beyond all the restrictions which are necessary to the birth of life and freedom, and of which the chief, and ultimately the only basis, are the commands of the conscience. Its aim contradicts the aim of conscience, and is not to promote evolution but to destroy it, and to rescue the individual soul from its dreary round. It substitutes for its constant vicissitudes of growth and decay an unchanging life, which is either far above it or far below. This constitutes its radical distinction from Stoicism, which also aims at the attainment of liberty but seeks it in compliance with the conscience, and does not see that, though that may give him freedom, it is through obedience to commands, even if they are those of his own conscience, and falls far short of perfect liberty. To be autonomous is not the same thing as to dispense with law. It is rather to submit to the strictest of laws, that is, the law of the conscience, which is none the less law because it is self-enacted.

FAITH WHICH TRANSCENDS MORALITY 201

All monastic bodies and associations, whatever their aim or name may be, are subject to rules: no two men can pursue a common end without them; but the principle of perfect liberty knows no law, and has no restraints, not even those of self-abnegation. The specific effect of this principle, when it is combined with the pure love of God, is to elevate the mind beyond all human obstacles, and make men wholly insensible of fear. Stoicism acts in the same direction, but it remains on earth and leaves intact the bonds of duty and personal honour; the perfect Christian already lives in Heaven, and knows nothing even of the highest earthly restrictions. He is completely indifferent to the ties of marriage and sonship and all home relationships, as well as to patriotism and to all human laws. The value of this temper in the early days of Christianity was inestimable, and the use of martyrs is not yet passed. They conquer the world by respect and not by fear, by spirit and not by force. The *sublimity* of Dante and Michael Angelo is due to this principle, and has no parallel in the art of the ancient world. And, as Longinus tells us, sublimity is the echo of a great soul, μεγάλης ψυχῆς ἀπήχημα.

Another result from the same temper is that it frees the mind from the influence of earthly ideals. The progress of the human race, as shown in history, is expressed and conditioned by the conflict of opposed ideals. The doctrine of the Kingdom of Heaven proclaims the vanity of all these ideals. If it were at once applied in human affairs it would not merely arrest evolution but extinguish the phenomenal world. And this is of course its purpose. Supported by the Kingdom on Earth, its effect is to raise the spirit of man to the greatest attainable height of grandeur. The function of a religion is to elevate the human mind, at whatever stage of evolution it may be. This can only be secured by setting the ideal beyond the limits of this world and freeing it of all objective content. All earthly ideals must sooner or later go out of fashion and lose their attraction. The Christian ideal is equally potent for the savage and for Sir Isaac Newton.

Points of Agreement and Difference between Christian and Scientific Principles

In its rejection of ethical values the doctrine of salvation by grace through faith resembles the spirit of science; and this leads to further points of resemblance. This form of religion, as we have seen, agrees with science in rejecting the efficacy of the human will. The essential meaning of sin is wilful disobedience to a Divine command. In the doctrine of God's Kingdom in Heaven there was one act of wilful disobedience, that is, by Adam ; but its effects were permanent, and except by the miracle of the Incarnation indelible. This doctrine knows of one offence and one miracle of redemption ; in the doctrine of works both sins and miracles are past counting. In the first, the personal responsibility ceased with the first sinner and did not descend to his progeny, who were the victims of sin as they were of disease, but not responsible : in the second they were both liable and responsible. Suffering, in the first, was the inevitable consequence of sin ; in the second a punishment which might be remitted on absolution. In these points science conforms with the doctrine of faith and contradicts the doctrine of works. The sin of Adam continues to infect the whole creation from its first occurrence to the end of the existence of the human race, and corresponds with the imaginary First Cause of Science. In the Kingdom on Earth even desire for forgiveness is a miracle, and an infringement of the natural law by which punishment is the necessary consequence of offence. Christianity, both in the one great miracle of redemption and in the daily miracles of confession and absolution, directly contradicts the oriental concept of Karma, or the πεπρωμένη of the Greeks.

We may continue our comparison with science. Not only do both it and the religious doctrine of faith reject the doctrine of free will, but, as a natural consequence, they further agree in allowing no place for human purpose. So far as human purpose goes, they agree in regarding it as wholly illusory. In the doctrine of faith the desire for worldly goods leads nowhere but to destruction, and is inspired by the Prince of Darkness. But though, logically, neither has within its earthly operation any kind of positive aim, the innate demand for a purpose, which shall distinguish and account for the relative values of the various kinds of action offered to our choice, asserts itself in both, and it is in their selection of a final end that science and Christianity differ, both in theory and in their practical effects on conduct. Nowhere else do we find a better illustration of the truth that the value of an ethical theory depends in no way on its logical consistency, but solely on the final end which it sets before men as the criterion of the relative values of conflicting lines of conduct. The ideal of science, so far as it has one, is its own perfection in this world, that is, the completion of our knowledge of law; the ideal of Christianity is perfect liberty, that is, the emancipation of life in another world.

The end of faith is Christ and his Heavenly Kingdom, an object far above all earthly ends: and though it agrees with science in rejecting human free will and human purpose, it asserts most strongly a Divine will, both of which are unknown and unintelligible to human faculties. We have just now observed that of all beliefs this is the most elevating and the most conducive to liberty; the earthly aim of pleasure which is the professed end of science is the most degrading, and leads most surely to slavery. The religious belief is strengthened on the emotional side of our nature by a love of God which absorbs the whole worshipper, and tends, unless kept under the control of dogma, to lose itself in a mysticism, which is essentially Pantheist. Science has no emotions, least of all a love of God.

Contrast of the Kingdom of Heaven with Earthly Philosophy

The doctrine of the Heavenly Kingdom is sharply divided both from Pantheism on the one hand and Utilitarianism on the other. It excludes the first by its assertion of the creation of the world out of nothing, and of its corruption through the fall of man, and by its theory of the influence of evil angels and demons; the second, by its insistence on obedience to the command of God as the sole criterion of goodness, its contempt for all cognizable ends of action, and its location of the final reward in a supra-sensible sphere of existence. In these respects it confirms the conclusions of a philosophy which postulates the reality of the distinction between good and evil, but is unable to discover in the material which is at its disposal, that is to say, within experience, any final end which may serve as a criterion to distinguish them. Increase of power, it will be remembered, is in some form or another the sole criterion of increase of life or forward evolution, and increase of life the sole end of virtuous or ethical action; but power, when left alone, turns against itself and destroys life. The doctrine of faith supplements this by agreeing that the final end of action is, humanly, unintelligible, and adds that it is in the mind of a personal God, who may and does communicate it in part to minds, to whom, for its own, and not for human, purpose, He chooses to reveal it; and it further agrees in placing the reward of true happiness beyond the confines of the senses.

We have seen that the pre-eminent merit of the dogma of perfect liberty in a future life, when humanly tested, is the perfect liberty and elevation of character resulting from a position which is raised above all earthly distinctions whatever. Its weakness is the necessary complement of its strength, and lies in its simplicity and want of comprehensiveness. In asserting the principle of perfect and unrestrained liberty it condemns law, and denudes human nature of what is virtually, while it is on earth, a half of its most valuable characteristics; that is to say, of all those qualities which render any degree of liberty possible, and keep it alive in a world of evolution by opposites. Inasmuch as the doctrine of redemption by faith gives expression to the principle of liberty in its utmost and transcendent purity, so it requires, for its counterpoise on earth, the expression of a supreme and transcendent authority. This is supplied in the Christian religion by the doctrine of the universal Church, and of Salvation by works, or of religious virtue. Our Lord, when he came, found both the Law and the Prophets; and their respective authorities were arranged in that order; the Law took the lead. His mission was not to destroy the Law, but to transpose the order of authority, placing liberty, that is to say the prophet, first, and above the priest. He was himself the last of the Prophets preceding his own reign on earth. This is indeed the essential characteristic of our religion: the preference of liberty above the law, but the equal maintenance of both while we are on earth, and the realization of the first in a changed life, and another world. The lamb led to the slaughter represents the Divine, the high priest on his throne the human side, of the Double-nature. We revere both, but the symbol of our worship is the crucifix and not the crosier.

The agreement in theory between the ethical and religious views is complete, so far as this life goes. Both demand, in the interests of life, a continual conflict between the two opposed principles of liberty and law, and both make liberty the leading principle, for the sake of which the support of law, or organic authority, is demanded. The condition in which authority is maintained for the sake of liberty is freedom: where liberty is subordinated to authority we get any degree of despotism, reaching to slavery, in which every trace of liberty is suppressed. Beyond this ethics cannot see. Freedom is the highest attainable earthly condition. Perfect liberty for all men neither is, nor, in existing conditions, ever can be, reached, or even approached beyond the limit of freedom; and freedom demands a certain balance not far removed from equality, between the conflicting principles of law and liberty. All this is confirmed in the Church by the rival theories of faith and works. What is added by Christianity is that, in another world, the leading principle of liberty shall exist in perfect purity, unclogged by the law on which it must lean on earth; and that faithful service on earth shall be rewarded in that world with a happiness that transcends pleasure and any other objects of our earthly desires.

Perfect liberty implies a complete emancipation

from the control of sensual attractions, and an entire devotion to the love of God. It is therefore practically impossible to men who are in possession of the means of enjoyment; it is equally impossible to those who are without them but desire to possess. Nearly all men fall into one or the other of these two categories, and, unless restrained by morality, will be guilty of excess. A religion that neglects or enfeebles the restraints of morality, even though it may offer a higher ideal, that is liberty, in its place, is acceptable only to a few minds of rare elevation. Among the multitude it may enjoy a brief and delusive popularity of enthusiasm, but it dies away almost immediately, leaving no traces but a permanent weakening of the bonds of morality. More usually it gives rise to small sects by a sudden burst of inspiration, which after a brief period of glowing heat dies down; and the sects are absorbed in the great mass from which they originally proceeded. Of this class may be reckoned the early Franciscans, the Jansenists, and the Quakers. Or, like the Wesleyans, and other of our Dissenters, they may voluntarily accept a separate organization of their own, and recognize both faith and works in varying proportions of value.

Doctrine of Salvation by Faith without Works necessarily unpopular

The doctrine of salvation by faith through grace is generally unacceptable. Its eschatological implications are not attractive. If salvation is confined rigorously to those who, by grace, are completely detached from earthly interests, experience shows, beyond mistake, that only a very minute minority are fitted to be saved. The great majority will refuse to apply this doctrine to their own cases, and will be unable to believe in a Deity whose omnipotence condemns nearly all his own creatures, including many of the highest moral deserts, to an after-life of endless torture. The assurance of an unknown design fails to make the prospect palatable, or reconcile it to their sense of justice; and no civilized man is able to worship what he can neither love nor respect. When a man, as may sometimes happen, is reconciled to the damnation of others by the assurance of his own salvation, he is guilty of the worst conceivable offence against the spirit of the religion of love.

The only test of a religion is its working. Unless its works, that is to say, is acceptable to a very large majority, it is not a religion; if it works evil, it is a superstition. By their fruits ye shall know them. The doctrine of faith without works fails in both respects. Except in unfrequent bursts of inspiration, it leaves the great majority of worshippers untouched, appealing only to minds of an uncommon type of elevation. In cases where it succeeds in imposing itself for a time on the masses, it becomes in its operation unmoral, acting in this respect in the same direction as science does. It deprives human nature of one of the latest and most valuable of its characteristics, its sense of right and wrong. A nation which is at the same time antinomian in its religious beliefs and scientific in its philosophy must very soon lose both its religious and its scientific capacities, to both of which morality is an essential support. It need not on that account be extinguished, but it will certainly fall to a lower level. It will contaminate its neighbours, and, should it prevail, it will bring about the destruction of contemporary civilization.

Compare Pantheism in India with Christianity

We may return for a moment to India. There too, as in Judea, the spirit of liberty and the spirit of law run in separate channels. The spirit of liberty is represented by the ascetics, of whom Buddha was the greatest. They recognized, with the Christian monk and the Hebrew prophet, that the worst form of slavery was subjection to desire

The escape they proposed was either with the Buddhist a final death and total annihilation or with the Brahmin the extinction of the separate personality by re-absorption in the universal spirit, from which it had originally proceeded as a separate spark from a bonfire. Their view of life is purely pessimist. All joy is evil in comparison with the peace which is the fruit of abstention. Their attitude towards law, as embodied in the religion of caste and its representatives, is indifferent, if not contemptuous. All social distinctions are unreal. The Brahmin is no better than the outcaste ; all men are equal, not only at birth, but throughout life, till death. The superiority which ascetics claim for themselves is one of a knowledge, which is real because it is realized in practice. This superiority they never assert : they are conscious of it ; and, where it is genuine, it is admitted everywhere, even by the Brahmins, who, while they accept their general views as to the real worthlessness of life, resemble the Christian Church in their recognition of the relative value of earthly distinctions, and make themselves, as the highest of all conceivable ranks, the equals of the Gods and a divine caste. In this they resemble the Jews, who regard themselves, in respect to all other races, as especially holy, or a race of priests ; but differ from them in taking a rank which is Divine and not priestly.

The difference is explained by the contradiction in their fundamental explanations of the nature of the universe. To the Hindu there was nothing beyond it, and no gap between the human and the Divine. His explanation therefore is philosophical and by metaphysics. To the Hebrew the explanation is religious. His God stands in the position of a creator, who might indeed create man in his own image, but who stood quite apart from and above him; who issued orders and punished disobedience. Men might fill the position of intermediaries or priests; but they could not bridge the gap. The bridge was at last furnished by the Incarnation of our Lord.

In India, the religion of law, as opposed to liberty, is expressed in the caste system, and the Brahminical caste is to that what the Church is to us. The resemblance is sufficiently near to induce casual observers to distinguish them as priests, but no one who has lived among them can admit a full identification. Their extravagant pretensions, as set forth in the Law of Manu, have only a faint reflection in common life. It is true that their claim to be equal with the Gods is admitted; but with a shade of irony, and they are employed in nearly every line of occupation, especially as cultivators and soldiers. They have no trace of a hierarchy: no one dreams of consulting them on questions of religious conscience, or confesses to them, or obtains their absolution from sin. They are not in charge of the worship of any particular God, least of all of Brahma, who is never the object of worship. They have no regular services or liturgies or ritual, and none of the ordinary apparatus of a priesthood. Their predominance is rather social than religious, and their magical participation in sacrifices is legendary and mythological rather than practical. When attached, as they occasionally are, to the service of a particular deity, they lose in rank among themselves and in the esteem of the outside public. Their dignity, both absolutely, as opposed to outsiders, and relatively among themselves, is purely hereditary, and is in no way dependent on their actions; though they may forfeit their caste by the neglect of caste rules.

These are the logical if not the universal results of a philosophic Pantheism, when it is applied to the affairs of daily life. If the only God is the pervading spirit of nature, life must exist either in this world or nowhere. No kind or number of metamorphoses will escape the round. The Gods themselves, so far as they are conceived as separate personalities, must be, and are, a part of the same perishing system. There is nothing absurd or impossible in making them equal with the Brahmins, or any other eminent individual or class. The system being self-contained, there can be no talk of inspiration from without in deciding the rival claims to election to eminence of worldly position, and the best available alternative is heredity. On that follows the hereditary distinction of the whole community into castes; at the beginning, the first four great divisions of Brahmins, soldiers, merchants, and cultivators, and, finally, the minute and complicated system of to-day, in which it is not always easy to detect the outline of the original classification. In order to remove all the temptations which are offered to discontent and personal ambition by the prospect of acquiring wealth, it is provided that the sole proprietor shall be the State, or, in this case, the hereditary King: an expedient which, without the King, is recommended by socialism in Europe with a similar purpose.

This amounts to one of the most complete victories of law over liberty that the world has ever seen. It is far removed from despotism, for the community is held together, not by fear, or by the will of a Despot, but by a well-understood system, in which each man has his rights and his appointed place; which they love, and for which they are willing to give their lives. Moreover the King himself, though honoured and obeyed with eager loyalty, has only the second place in the social order, and is overshadowed by the Brahmins, whose plain interest lies in the maintenance of a system to which they owe their own predominance. The defect of liberty is a fatal bar to development, and that is probably the only serious objection to which the system itself is liable. From the point of view of pleasure and pain it compares favourably with others. The opportunities of obtaining pleasure are pretty evenly distributed, but neither pleasure nor pain is greatly desired or feared, and both remain at the same level. It does not exclude internal war, for the states become small, and are apt to fight on trifling differences: against hostile aggression from without it presents an almost impenetrable barrier. To its own members it is eminently humane; and if its treatment of outcastes be objected to, it must be remembered that they do not belong to it; that they are the descendants of a conquered race; and that if they are allowed to live it is by an act of grace, and they must, like the Gibeonites, be kept in subjection.

The spirit of liberty, which, here as in Christianity, has its home outside the regular organism in the ranks of the ascetics, makes itself felt within that organism by a very low valuation of all personal luxuries, and particularly of money as the general means of procuring them. On the other hand, they can point to no eternal world beyond this life of continual flux and change. They offer no alternative either bad or good, to the existing dispensation, and exempt it alike from the fear of disruption through private covetousness, and the hope of advance through individual self-sacrifice to a public ideal. Neither bad motives nor good disturb their content with their present social conditions. The absence of a good ambition which may lead, through self-devotion, to a higher stage of life is the necessary result of a Pantheism which confines the future prospects of both individuals and communities to the present course of nature, and is unable to raise them above it. Any natural philosophy or scientific metaphysics which denies a supernatural religion and tries to usurp its place must have the same effect, and act as a check on the advance of humanity. The contempt of money, which is the good result, is a part of the general aversion to sensual pleasure, which is common to all ascetics, Hindu and Christian alike. It is one of the principal dangers of clericalism that it is apt to make terms with metaphysics. It thereby ceases to be Christian, or to serve the purpose of Christianity. It becomes Hindu in its aversion to advance; without the contempt for money which is a preservative against decay.

LIBERTY
THE KINGDOM ON EARTH

LIBERTY

THE KINGDOM ON EARTH

Equal Growth of Opposites

IN its scale of the moral values the principal change effected by Christianity was the reversal of the relative positions of justice and love, that is, of law and of liberty. Both were highly valued in the old dispensation, but the first was essentially the virtue of the priestly government, whereas love inspired the prophets, and only took the first place when they definitely acquired the lead. Even the prophets admitted, as a rule, the supremacy of the law. 'Populus tuus omnes *iusti*, in perpetuum hereditabunt terram' (Isaiah lx. 21) gives the key-note of Jewish morality, and should be contrasted with the second beatitude, 'Beati mites; quoniam ipsi possidebunt terram'. The Kingdom of earth is promised by Isaiah to the just; by our Lord, to the merciful. The Christian promise is anticipated in Psalm xxxvii (xxxvi). 11: 'Mansueti autem hereditabunt terram'; but that never truly represented the dominant aspiration of the Jewish nation. The reign of justice is an immense advance on the primitive rule of force, and it is promised not only permanence but increase of strength in this world. 'Minimus erit in mille, et parvulus in fortissimam gentem.'

The most abstract meaning of justice is equality between conflicting opposites. That is the essential principle of the law of life on earth. Life depends, in the first place, on what may be called an instability in the balance through which first one side and then the other gains a slight advantage over exact equilibrium. The two universal elements in the struggle under which all the minor elements may be classed are good and evil. The struggle is between the hosts of the angels of light and the hosts of the angels of darkness. On earth the struggle is still undecided. Neither host has gained a decisive advantage. Every slight advantage to the principle of light is an increase of life; to the principle of darkness, disappearance of light: for light and life are the same thing. The earth, as the scene of life, is the battle-field. As long as evolution continues, so long will the conflict endure. The aim of man on earth is not a final decision but a continual growth of light, which is conditioned by a parallel growth of darkness.

In one respect this metaphor fails. It does not account for the principle of growth, that is to say, of evolution. In ordinary conflicts there are casualties, and the opponents on both sides are weakened. In this, both sides gain, in numbers and in other sources of strength.

Origin of Evil

Of the origin of evil we are given no explanation. The principle of disobedience was active in creation before the appearance of man. It was communicated by the Serpent to the woman, and proceeded upwards from one of the lower orders of animal, through the inferior partner in the pair of men, to the head of all created things. The reasons by which Eve justified her disobedience were of precisely the same class as would satisfy a modern philosopher. She saw that the tree was good to eat, and fair to the eyes, and delightful to look on (*aspectuque delectabile*), and she took the fruit thereof and did eat. Her view was strictly utilitarian. The reason given by the Creator for his prohibition is that He wished men to remain in ignorance of good and evil. After the transgression it was carried down till the end of time by inheritance. This then, the continuance of evil in opposition to good in the economy of the earth, is the Divine Justice. Evil, in order to maintain its position in the economy, must remain nearly even with good, and can neither disappear nor become negligible.

No account is given of the real origin of sin. An attempt is made to carry it beyond the limits of creation by representing the snake as inspired by or as a personification of an evil spirit; and further intercourse between angels and women is mentioned; but the rebellion of the angels is only explained by attributing to them the evil impulses of mankind, such as pride and envy. The question is put back into the region of the unknown; it is not solved. The fact remains that the justice which keeps an even hand between good and evil, and pleasure and pain, though it complies with the human form of the concept, and though it is the necessary condition of man's survival and advance in this world, need not extend beyond the world of change, and has no explanation either within that world or beyond it, either in reason or in revelation. This, which is the view of a reasonable philosophy, deprives the whole creation of all absolute value, while it maintains within creation the supreme, and indeed exclusive, importance of the moral values. So far as reason has authority, the entrance of a soul into life, or its departure through death, are matters of no consequence. What gives life consequence is the observance, during the interval, of the moral law. The soul enters into the world of law and of life through the gate of birth; and its aim is, through the observance of the law, to pass through the gates of death into the world where there is life but no law.

The Two Kingdoms

But Morality requires a single final end, and for that it must select between obedience to law, that is to say, no external end, but itself only, and life, or its own contrary.

The answer given by Christianity is twofold, according as it comes from the point of view of faith or of works, and each of the answers, when taken by itself, contradicts the other. Each, taken by itself, would be fatal to the survival of the religion on earth; the two, taken together, make the strongest religion that has ever existed, or that we can conceive. The religion of the Jews asserted salvation by works only, coupled with belief in one God, the Creator and Ruler of all things. Our Lord retained that wholly, ' Not one jot or one tittle of the law shall pass away '. But He added, above and beyond the divine Kingdom on earth, another Kingdom in Heaven, where Law will no longer survive, but only love and liberty. At the same time He completed the divine law on earth, by adding that, of the two principles of control and love, the equal conflict between which constitutes earthly justice, love must take the first place, leaving it to be inferred that law is only valuable as the means to love.

The Kingdom of God in Heaven, and the doctrine

of Salvation by faith, have no concern with justice. Men who are already saved will no doubt be perfectly virtuous, but faith and repentance come by the free unearned gift of grace. That gift is not deserved by anything a man can do. It has been decided for each individual from eternity by an irrevocable decree. Neither in Heaven nor in earth is there any room for the human form of justice, nor of any human principle whatever except the love of God for his creatures, and the same love reflected in the mind of the creatures whom He has saved. So far is the gift from being given as a reward for works that its message is addressed in the first place to sinners. Something has been already said of the dangers of this doctrine. By excluding the authority of law and duty, and proclaiming a perfect liberty, it may indeed raise men for a time to a condition that is higher than virtue; but no society can endure without law, and there is no good law without justice.

The principle of justice, though alien to the doctrine of faith, and superseded in that by the principle of love, was given as dominant a position in the doctrine of works as it had previously held in the Jewish religion from which that doctrine was derived. If we compare it with the Justice of morality we find that the Christian belief agrees with the latter in its leading principles and its distinctions. Ethics recognized two forms of social justice, the distributive and the retributive. Distributive justice consists in impartial recognition, in the distribution of good things, of both of the conflicting principles of numbers and quality. That is to say, in distributing freedom, it pays an equal attention to the claim of the multitude that each man shall receive an equal share, without inquiry into merit; and to the claim of the superior individual that the share of each man shall be in accordance with his deserts. Both of these are forms of justice: they are universal and contradictory. The other, that is, retributive justice, is concerned with the award of evil things in return for evil acts. What it demands is that, in criminal sentences, there should be an equality between the penalty and the moral indignation which is excited by the crime. Both demand a complete equality of person before the law. A judge, in order to be just, must be indifferent to pity, respect, and fear and love and hatred. The parties must come before him as unqualified ciphers. Through all these forms, and in every other sense in which the word can be used, justice is always equality. The aim of the just man is to maintain equality. 'Si fractus illabatur orbis, impavidum ferient ruinae.' To maintain this end is life; to substitute another is death. Security of person and property may be the result, but to substitute as our end what one believes to secure that result is like substituting happiness for virtue in the guidance of conduct. The end in both cases is surely missed. That end is indeed nothing beyond continued life and growth in an unknown future, and in no sense of the word utilitarian—Utilitarianism is agnostic, and takes no account of an unknown future, or of anything that is unknown.

All these concepts appear in the teaching of the Church. The doctrine of the absolute equality of all men as the sons of God is proclaimed with a force and directness which have led many Churchmen to select it as the distinctive doctrine of Christianity. That it is not, for it is held in common with Islam and with Buddhism. But though it is certainly one of the leading doctrines, it does not prevent God's dealing with men in accordance with their deserts. He visits the sins of the fathers upon the children unto the third and fourth generation of them that hate him, and shows mercy unto thousands of them that love him and keep his commandments, and so to the end of the Bible. The God of the Apocalypse is as conspicuous for His wrath against the heathen world as He is for His love for the saints. The doctrine of retributive justice has never been more strongly asserted. St. Augustine says, ' Peccator eras ; confitere, ut sis iustus', identifying justice or justification with virtue. This is the maxim of the Kingdom on Earth; but the Kingdom of Heaven puts love above justice.

The Church of Rome

The contrary needs of distributive justice are supplied in the constitution of the Roman Church. This has a strictly democratic basis, all believers being theoretically equal and with equal claims to any office of any rank within the Church, from the highest to the lowest, without any preference for worldly rank or position at birth. It culminates in a single ruler with absolute power, and a judgement which is exempted from human criticism; and this ruler is appointed not by man but by the voice of God, which makes itself heard in a small college of ecclesiastical princes. Between that and the laymen, all of whom, from the slave to the highest noble, are exactly equal before God, is arranged the vast hierarchy of the Priesthood; and in this, again, every appointment is made for no other consideration but personal merit. The existence of merit is indicated by divine inspiration, and it may not be controverted, least of all by the laity. The need of excluding other and less worthy motives is reflected in the genuine horror of simony, that is, the communication of the Spirit in exchange for gifts. By this horror the prophet Savonarola was inspired, and his murder by a simoniacal Pope was one of the heaviest blows which has ever been inflicted on Christianity.

The combination of complete individual equality with rewards for personal merit, in which merit is secured, as far as may be, against the disturbing influence of mammon, realizes, in a way that has never been seen elsewhere, the theoretical needs of political justice, and it has given life to an institution of unequalled endurance and efficiency. The Roman Church conforms in its constitution with the demands of an abstract philosophy, and it has administered affairs of supreme importance, in every quarter of the globe, with a rigid unity of purpose, an unselfish devotion on the part of its servants, a width and accuracy of knowledge, and a minuteness of sympathy, such as have been the endowment of no other organization. It has maintained a complicated doctrine, has successfully resisted schism from within and external enemies, and is as young now as it was in the times of its greatest strength, with unexhausted power both of internal development and of resistance to hostile aggression.

The principle of liberty then is asserted in a form that is absolute and universal in the doctrine of faith, that is, of the kingdom of Heaven: the principle of authority is asserted, in a form that is equally absolute and universal, in the doctrine of works, or of the Kingdom on Earth. The doctrine of the earthly Kingdom may be traced, like the other, to the promise to Eve, at the commencement of man's life of labour. It assumed its specific shape, as invested in the Jewish nation, in the covenant with Abraham, and from that time till to-day it has remained the dominant ideal which has guided the course of Jewish history.

Universality of the Earthly Kingdom

Like those of the doctrine of faith, the aims of the doctrine of works are universal. All races of men are to be saved by inclusion in the Kingdom. The form in the Jewish and the Christian Churches is the same, but the details differ widely. The son of David is a man; the Son of God, both Man and God. The Kingdom, that is, the seat of final salvation, is, for the Jew, in this world; for the Christian, in the next. Of many divergent pictures of the Jewish Apocalypse, the following may be taken as typical. The Messianic King is the ninth in succession after Nimrod, Joseph, Solomon, Ahab, Nebuchadnezzar, Cyrus, and Alexander; and, like them, human.[1] The first and the last were God.

[1] *The Pirke of Rabbi Eleazar* (Friedlander), p. 80.

232 UNIVERSALITY OF EARTHLY KINGDOM

The reign of the Messiah was to be universal but not eternal. The only eternal form of monarchy was God's, that is, a Theocracy. The Messiah was merely a man like his predecessors, and like the Mahdi of Islam. He was a great conqueror, and his reign ends after 1,000 years, when he surrenders it to God.

The Jews lay great stress on the Universality of their Kingdom. All men alike are to be admitted to its privileges, but not on equal terms. The Jews are to remain the priestly caste throughout. Peace and plenty were to be common to all, but the holy people were to be the ministers for the servants of God, with all the privileges attached to that eminence. This, briefly, was the ideal of the Jewish Kingdom on earth. A Jewish King of the lineage of David, with the Jewish people as sole ministers of the Law, who, after putting down all enemies, should restore the government to God and do away with the rule of many which has ensued on the curse of Babel.[1] All national distinctions were to be merged in a universal Judaism, but the Jews were to retain the supremacy and the government.

These promises of an earthly kingdom were confirmed in the second (Vulgate order) beatitude. Unlike the Kingdom of Heaven, where the gift to the

[1] *Pirke*, p. 177.

poor in spirit is immediate ('theirs *is* the Kingdom of the Heavens'), the inheritance of the earth is promised in the future to the merciful ('they *will* obtain it'). The implication was that the gift would be realized at the second coming, which, at the time, was believed to be very near; within the lifetime of some that stood by, though our Lord Himself disclaimed all exact knowledge. In the meantime the custody of the faith and the administration ('feed my sheep') of the spiritual needs of the disciples were entrusted to the apostles with St. Peter at their head, and they were given full power to bind and to release.

Development of the Doctrine of Works necessitated by the delay of the Second Coming

It is impossible to give even a cursory account of these all-important events without appearing to express an opinion on questions of faith, which are still debated. No such questions could have arisen in the first century of our era, but the unexpected course of history and the necessary development of dogma in reaction to constantly changing surroundings have made them inevitable. An ethical philosopher is justified in regarding as Christian any body of men whose faith affects history in the direction which is peculiar to Christianity; that is to say, in the establishment of a belief which combines a perfect freedom with an absolute authority, and makes a transcendental liberty the final end to which all the services of authority are to be directed. Perfect *freedom* is secured on Earth by the authority of the Church and a life in accordance with the divine law; perfect *liberty* is secured in the minds of saints, and in the world to come, by the Kingdom of Heaven and a life of faith. The two are so intimately blended that it is impossible to distinguish them except in theory. In practice, they cannot be separated. There are no good works without sanctification, and no salvation without faith. What distinguishes Christianity from Judaism is the reversal of the relative positions of liberty and law, and the establishment of the former as the final end of human action. The Pantheist religions of India make liberty their final end, but have no Church and no faith in works; Islam has a lively faith in authority but none in liberty; neither has been able to advance beyond a fixed point in civilization. Christianity has not only advanced much farther than either, but its prospects of further advance are, owing to the completeness and the supernatural character of its final end, unlimited.

Kingdom on Earth continuation of Jewish Church, with modifications

The Kingdom on Earth, of which at His appearance our Lord will be both King and High Priest, is the survival, with modifications, of the Jewish Church. Like that, it is divided into two classes, the Priests and the Laity. The Church contained no priestly tribe by whom the office could descend by heredity, and the mode of election varied from the earliest times; but the appointment was held to be ultimately by the voice of God, making itself heard by His people or their representatives. This was the first and principal modification. It introduced a democratic element of varying strength into the government of the Church. It was where the constitution was most similar in form that the resemblance in spirit was nearest. The spiritual aristocracy at Rome, under its single Pontiff, reproduced with a close approach to fidelity the Sanhedrin at Jerusalem with its High Priest; and they were like in the elevation of their worldly ambitions, in the nobility of their architecture, the splendour and solemnity of their robes and ritual, their vigilant care of the people, and the merciless severity with which they measured out torture, shame, and death to their enemies :

'Benigne a' suoi, ed a' nimici crude.'

The basis of the morality of the Church was the Mosaic Law. This was modified by the teaching of the Gospel, in much the same way as it had previously been modified by the prophets and tradition; but more radically. There was no discontinuity or breach in growth, and the change was hardly greater than what comes over every one when from boy he becomes man. In the same way as the God of the Jews was still, though explained as a Trinity, the God of the Christian, so the sole basis of morality in both was the inscrutable will of God, which was explained, in the latter dispensation, by a universal love for mankind. Christian morality is no independent growth, no Minerva sprung full armed from the head of God. It is a legitimate development from the law of Moses, and only as such can it be understood.

Patriotism

The direction of growth, and the kind of transformation which ensued, can be traced in the case of patriotism. Of this, which was the first of all the virtues of antiquity, no mention is made in Christianity, and by many it is believed to have become obsolete. This is a mistake: it still survives, but in a changed form; and the change has been in strict conformity with the ethical laws of evolution: that is to say, in the direction of growth, or increasing width of comprehension. It should be remembered that the principle of common self-sacrifice on the part of all the members of a community did not always, or originally at all, apply to a State, in the form of a modern nation. Patriotism took its rise in the tribe or the city, or any body of men who were united under a single government. The motive for their sacrifice was always freedom, or the power to live in the way they chose and follow the lines for the prosecution of which they were associated. What they fought for was not their country but their common ideal: at first for its maintenance, and afterwards, obeying a universal law of evolution, for its developments and expansion beyond its original frontiers. Some men were agriculturists, others hunters; the ideals came into conflict, and there was war. Cain slew his brother Abel. The ideal of Sparta was military; of Athens, commercial; and so on.

No one can deny to the Jews the possession of this virtue. It is the intensity of their patriotism that distinguishes them from all other nations, and to that they owe it that they have survived the captivities of Egypt and Babylon and the contempt and ill-usage of the last two thousand years; and still remain a separate people, continually increasing in numbers and wealth and power. Under the

Maccabees, and on many other occasions, it has inspired them with a heroism that has never been excelled, and there is no reason to suppose that even now it has lost its force. No other nation has ever surpassed them in the hatred and contempt they felt for foreigners, or in the atrocity of their dealings with them, and no one who knows anything of the modern Jew will believe that they have gained in their respect for strangers. They resent all alien mixture in board and bed, and are, and always have been, attached to the ideal of their tribe with a passion that has never been paralleled in strength and tenacity. That ideal was and still is religion: the worship of one God without an image, and obedience to His law. The love of their country, strong though it is, has always been weak in comparison with their devotion to their law.

The feeling has descended to the Christian Church in undiminished strength: but its scope of application has been greatly enlarged, and the ideal transformed. The scope of Jewish patriotism was originally all the twelve tribes that claimed descent from Israel. After the captivity it became, in practice, narrowed to the single tribe of Judah, with its adherents among the Levites, and a remnant from the north of Palestine. The writer of this is, on his mother's side, in part, an Israelite of the tribe of Napthali. When the lamp of the law was handed over to the Church, this narrowing basis was suddenly expanded, and embraced the whole body of believers. All other distinctions were swept away. There was no longer Jew or Gentile, bond or free, man or woman, but all were one in the Unity of the Church. But all who were outside that limit occupied the same position with regard to the Church as the Gentile did, and still does, in regard to the Jewish community; and were treated with the same rigour. Charity and humility were for believers only, and did not extend beyond them. Its persecuting tendency was inherited by the Church from the Jews; its detachment from tribal interests, by the revolution which was made by Christianity, removed all obstacles which might have stood in the way of extending its dominion by proselytism. Its only limit became the acceptance of its faith. It became potentially universal; and only waited to become so in practice for the time when all dissent, whether within the countries in which it was recognized as the ruling belief, or beyond them, was extinguished. The Church became the Israel of God.

Universal Final End of the Patriotism of the Church

Its dominion must always remain purely religious and spiritual. It is obvious that a patriotism thus extended, must, unless very strictly defined, run counter to the ethical patriotism, which has for its centre the nation. The necessary definition is supplied by the consideration that, being a religious patriotism, it must restrict its sympathies and its active interference to religious aims. In a war when one side is admittedly Christian and the other represents a hostile belief, as, for instance, in the Crusades, there will be no difficulty. Every ounce of the power of the Church will be thrown on the side of the Christian. Since the revival of nations, and the national spirit, on the final disappearance of Roman universalism in the sixteenth century, the case has become much more complex. The clue is to be found in the consideration that the ideal of Christianity is a perfect liberty. That is not attainable on earth, but the aim of the Church is the highest form of freedom, that is to say, that compromise between law and liberty which constitutes order, and is the condition under which the greatest possible degree of liberty can be secured and maintained in this world.

From this premise several conclusions may be deduced. The first is that the sympathies of the Church must always be opposite to every form either of anarchy or of despotism. By despotism is not meant a monarchial government which represents the nation and is accepted as its representative by

PATRIOTISM OF THE CHURCH

the people. That is not opposed to freedom. On the other hand, anarchy certainly includes a state of things where the people are impatient of control by a free government; or desire to merge distinctions due to merit in a perfect equality, and thereby outrage Justice; or are so effeminate as to be unable to face the sterner aspects of life. All these lead through anarchy to slavery. Again it will resent all attempts of interference by one State with the internal affairs of another, unless they are justified by the necessity of self-defence. Least of all will it sympathize with the ambition of a universal empire. That, when realized, would, by extinguishing war, put an end to freedom, and rob humanity of half its noblest qualities. If it were in fact the case that Christianity is indifferent to forms of government, it would rightly be called the religion of slaves; but that charge is brought against it most frequently by men who have rejected the Kingdom of works, and are, on that very account, unable to retain the Kingdom of faith. The two stand and fall together.

The Church on Earth then, though its mission excludes it from direct participation in political and national movements, must, so far as it is inspired by the doctrine of works, be in active sympathy with the highest of the tendencies of political morality, that is, with patriotism. Its own aim is spiritual freedom, and that does not for long survive political freedom. The aim in both cases is the same, that is, the elevation of character and aim, or ideal, over large masses of men who are united together for a single purpose. That is, so far as evolution admits of being personified, one of the purposes of evolutionary progress, or growth, and it is of increasing importance in a period which seems to rate the growth of the community at a higher value than the development of the individual. It is an essential truth, which must never be lost sight of, that the freedom of political institutions, and the personal freedom of the individuals to which they apply, are inseparable, and that no State can be free unless it is composed of citizens each of whom is in free subjection to the law of his own conscience.

This is not true of the doctrine of faith, taken by itself and without reference to the doctrine of works. Salvation by faith is, as we have seen, an unconditional gift, decreed before the beginning of time by the inexplicable will of God. It denies all efficacy to the human will, and cuts away the basis of morality. It assures to the individual a perfect liberty; and that can only be attained by a complete rejection of all social interests. It is essentially the religion of the individual, and, where held by large numbers, it goes far to incapacitate them for political independence. It is not incompatible with any earthly conditions. Slavery does not extinguish it: indeed the annihilation through bondage of the independent will in the activities of this life, even when it is involuntary, runs along parallel lines, and in the same direction. The torments of bondage are no worse than what are supported by the ascetic, and, when willingly accepted, have the same result. The consciousness of this is a perfect consolation, and reconciles a man to his lot, turning his slavery into a perfect liberty. Indeed, this form of belief when taken by itself may justly be called the religion of slaves. And that is not wholly a reproach. If it fails in making good citizens, it produces the highest possible individual characters under all conditions, even the lowest and most unfavourable. But only a few are selected for this grace; the masses must be ruled by morality.

Function of the Church to preserve the Truth by Teaching

The distinctive function of both the Jewish and Christian Kingdoms on Earth was to preserve and interpret the law of God, and to enforce its observance by the people. It was this claim that explains the intolerance of the Church of Rome, during the Middle Ages, of the teaching by laymen, which was asserted as a right by the 'Friends of God' and other quasi-mystical sects. It was treated as heresy, and its assertion was punished by death at the stake. The conflict was between the prophet and the priest, the Kingdom of God in Heaven and His Kingdom on Earth. In the earlier stages of the conflict the position of the Church was doubtful and undecided. Eckhart, the most learned and most inspired of the prophets, occupied a high position in the order of Dominican monks. Tauler, a learned priest of the same order, was allowed to defy the Papal interdict and administer the consolations of religion in a tract where they were forbidden: the chief of the secret order of 'Friends of God', himself a layman, sought an audience of the Pope, was kindly received, and was commended by him to the care of the local Bishop. But, eventually, the ordinary officials of the Church burned the same man at the stake, with all his followers. His crime was that, like George Fox, and St. Paul before them both, he asserted that he was in Christ, and Christ in him.

Love of God and Love of Man

While, in the Kingdom of faith, the whole of goodness was subsumed in the motive of Love of God, the same office was taken in the Kingdom of earth by the Love of man. Theoretically, man may be identified with God, and the two concepts of Love of God and love of man may be regarded as the same thing; but, if a doctrine is to be judged by its fruits, the practical meaning is quite distinct, and even opposite. And there is the following theoretic distinction. If the love of God and the love of man are the same thing, it is because the whole of the Faithful are the sons of God, and the members of His Church, which is the body of Christ. The definition, thus narrowed, would exclude the heathen. But the love which was preached in the Gospel, though at first confined to the Jews, was primarily to the sinners among them; and it was finally extended to all nations.

The practical effect on conduct is, logically, opposite. The love of God is the strongest rational motive for avoiding human society and abstention from human affairs. All contact with them is a distraction, and a pure concentration can only be gained in the desert, or on the elevation of a pillar. The love of man, on the contrary, is a motive to seek their society, and to take as great a part as possible in their affairs. St. Anthony the great, and, still better, St. Simeon Stylites represented the first; St. Boniface and St. Bernard, the second. A brief comparison of the effects on history of each of these ideals will be necessary to our design.

The effect on character of each ideal is opposite,

and neither, by itself, will be accepted as being in harmony with any ideal that has been evolved from the dictates of morality. We may take as a fairly accurate description of the logical outcome of the doctrine of faith by grace, Professor Harnack's account of the ideal of the Greek Church. 'The man who practises silence and purity, who shuns not only the world, but also the Church of the world, who avoids not only false doctrine, but any statement about the true, who fasts, gives himself to contemplation, and steadily waits for God's glorious light to dawn upon his gaze; who attaches no value to anything except tranquillity and meditation on the eternal, who asks nothing of life but death, and in such complete unselfishness and purity discovers the fountains of mercy—this is the Christian. To him not even the Church, or the consecration which it bestows, is an absolute necessity. For such a man the whole system of sanctified secularity has vanished.'[1] Another passage from the same author may be quoted: 'Ask either the Greek or the Roman Church in what consists the most perfect Christian life, and both will reply: in the service of God, by the renunciation of all the goods of this life, of property, of marriage, of personal will and personal honour, in short, in religious retirement

[1] A. Harnack, *What is Christianity?* p. 242.

LOVE OF GOD AND LOVE OF MAN 247

from the world, in Monasticism. The true Monk is the true and most perfect type of a Christian.'[1]

Professor Harnack clearly points out with regard to the first of these pictures that the resemblance is one-sided, and misses the full spirit of Christianity. It is in fact as good a portrait of a Hindu ascetic as of a Christian saint. What distinguishes good from evil in Ethical inquiries is the aim towards which any line of conduct is directed. Taking a purely moral view of religion, we may say that the immediate result of asceticism is strength of character. This, however, is not its final end; for strength of character may be devoted to any end, whether it be good or evil. Strength becomes good only when it is devoted to a good end; and the good immediate end in religion is elevation of character. Elevation of character depends not so much on strength as on the aim, and this is the point on which the Hindu and the Christian ascetic differ most materially. The aim which actuates the Hindu is pure nihilism. He is convinced of the radical badness of life on earth, and, being further convinced of his own immortality, he desires to escape from active life into a state of pure, unqualified existence. The Christian, on the contrary, while equally sure of the evil in our present life, is at the same time assured of another life of perfect

[1] Id., *Das Mönchtum, Reden und Aufsätze*, i. 83.

blessedness, which may be attained as a reward for the renunciation of the seeming goods of this world. His motive is the love of God, which is the necessary return of God's proved love for him. Beyond his fear and hatred of this life the Hindu ascetic has no motive.

Thus, the Christian Kingdom of Heaven substitutes for the motive of the Hindu another and much higher motive of its own. It replaces the hatred of the world by the love of God. The first cannot fairly be called degrading in itself: it leads to strength of character, but no farther. It leaves the soul in a vacuum, with no motive whereby to give a direction to its forces. It has two main alternative issues. The devotee may either abandon the practice of self-torment and return to the world, strengthened and purified; or may retain it till his powers break and he becomes imbecile. It is true of the Hindu ascetic, but not equally true of the Christian, that the whole system of sanctified secularity is to him as nothing. The man who has abandoned the world stands separate from the caste system, and above it. He is, moreover, above and indifferent to all the rules of morality.

Much of this is true of the Christian saint as we find him in actual life. But the whole character is coloured and elevated by being suffused with the highest of the moral motives, and under its guidance.

The high abstraction of the love of God is itself a guarantee of the highest attainable elevation of mind in the man who can attain it, and though it may, and does, transcend all the rules of morality, it creates an atmosphere in which no bad growth can flourish. It rejects all that is mean and degrading. The incalculable moral value of a supersensuous love was apparent to minds of the philosophic elevation of Plato and Spinoza. With the author of Deuteronomy, it was the first religious duty, and comprehended all others, but it reaches its highest range and intensity when it is paid to a Being who is both God and Man, for benefits, both in this life and in the next, which are too great to be returned. It is this love, and not asceticism, that distinguishes the Christian saint from the Hindu devotee. With the Christian it transforms his whole nature, and gives him a new life: the Hindu is entirely without it.

Indeed, the quality of a complete remoteness from the world, including 'the whole system of sanctified secularity', is far more truly characteristic of the Hindu ascetic than of the Christian saint. The practical religious system in India is the institution of castes, with its appropriate range of values beginning with disgust and contempt for the maker of shoes and culminating in the semi-worship which is paid to a Brahmin. This the man who has conquered the world utterly rejects. The Brahmin and the cobbler are to him of exactly equal value. The secular institutions in Christianity which correspond to the caste system is the Church, and this, I venture to assert, no Christian saint ever wholly escapes. The maxim, 'Nulla salus extra ecclesiam', applies to him as well as to all others, and, however complete his renunciation of the world may be, it is impossible for him to renounce his religious duties without ceasing to be a Christian. To the Hindu, on the contrary, the Gods themselves are a part of the world, and in renouncing the world he renounces them. The only real divinity remains himself.

Moreover, though it has been adopted as their own by many professing Christians, and has been sanctioned in many single instances by its corporate authority, the pure ascetic ideal, such as flourishes in India, never has been, and never could be, accepted as its own by the Church as a whole. It is, indeed, in its spirit, Doketic, and overlooks the human nature of Christ. In the perfect concept, man claims an equal love and service with God, and the two, though conceptually distinguishable, may not be divided in practice. Christ's representative on earth is the Church. In that resides His Earthly Kingdom, and, to the true Christian, love and service for the visible Church on earth are, though ideally separate, practically identical with love and service of God in His heavenly Kingdom. The doctrine of faith is true in itself, but not by itself. It is the highest part of Christianity and its distinctive feature; but it does not constitute a complete Christian ideal until it is joined with the old Jewish doctrine of works.

Secondary Aims of the Church

The aim of the Church was to justify its title of Catholic by becoming truly universal. Its ideal was and is universal spiritual dominion, and its efforts took two main directions: first, the conversion of the heathen, and, secondly, the prevention of internal disruption. Under the second head came the elaboration and maintenance of the vast organism which constitutes the body of the Church, and the care and circulation of its life blood, the doctrine. The first element in the doctrine which it was its duty to promulgate abroad and preserve at home was the Divine nature of Christ; the second was His human nature as the Jewish Messiah, and included the whole of the Law and the prophets, which were the law on which the very existence of the Church depended. This aspect of the case fully justified the claim of early Christians that the Old Testament was given not for the Jews but for themselves. Taken by itself it is a body of rules and examples without unity of purpose. The New Testament gives it a single purpose, and in conjunction with that it becomes a complete system. This is a sufficient answer to the objection which contrasts Christianity as a religion of orthodoxy or right opinion with Judaism as a religion of orthopraxy or right action. It is as much a religion of right action as Judaism itself. Not one jot or tittle of the Law is allowed to drop ; that will last as long as the heavens and the earth endure ; but it completes the law by giving it a further object in a Kingdom of God which is beyond this universe, and in the hearts of saints who are already free from the bondage of worldly ties. That kingdom already exists in the soul of the saint, and it will last when the heavens and the earth have ceased to be.

By accepting the ascetic ideal as its own, Christianity would contradict the example of its Divine Model, and exclude the whole of His mission except the temptation in the wilderness. Again, in St. Paul's life the only period of interest would be his sojourn in Arabia. To neither of these episodes does the holy record attach a greater importance than the biography of a conqueror does to his days at a preparatory school ; nor indeed

SECONDARY AIMS OF THE CHURCH

do they possess any superior interest in comparison with the events of their years of active work. If we want to detect the actual ideal of the western Church we need only regard the lives of those whom she has singled out as saints. They have been distinguished in nearly every line of practical achievement. The interests of that Church reached into every branch of life, and its saints came from all ranks and every profession. Kings and knights and statesmen, scholars and divines, besides the martyrs, who belong to no special class and of whom a large number were soldiers in the ranks; all indeed who have served her by any special act of self-sacrifice.

If we are to regard the official title of sanctity as expressing in any way the ideals of the Church, we are compelled to admit that an active life of service to the Church was the primary qualification for it, and that, though in exceptional cases an indolent ascetic may have gained the honour, the task of subduing the flesh has been mainly valued as a training for the production of the highest forms of courage, devotion, and elevation of character, which are required for conduct in difficult circumstances. This merely reflects human nature, which, at its best, is impatient of greatness when it is not displayed in action affecting others. St. Celestine, before he was canonized, was made the object of his fierce contempt by the most sublime of the poets of all ages :

> Fama di loro il mondo esser non lassa,
> Misericordia e Giustizia gli sdegna:
> . . . .
> Che fece per viltate il gran rifiuto.

Even in India human nature is not very dissimilar, and the love and respect of the people is paid to the man who returned from the wilds, victorious over himself and the messenger of peace to his neighbours, as Gotama Buddha was of old and many still are. The ascetic who mixes with them to display his contempt for their religious observances is rewarded by their fear and aversion. From the examples that have illustrated our own religion we need only select the equal lights of St. Francis and St. Dominic. The true monk, in order to become a saint, must be much more than a mere monk ; he must also be a man of the world.

Love and Liberty

What made love the distinctive mark of prophecy was that it is the mental affection that is bound up with liberty. Liberty means unrestricted activity in the pursuit of an end, and love is the emotion which assists the person who is beloved in that pursuit. When a man loves himself he devotes all his energy or activity to the pursuit of his own personal ends : self-love is self-assertion. When he loves his neighbour, and so far as he loves him, his energy is applied to the attainment of his neighbour's ends. The circle widens, and the patriot or lover of his country devotes himself and all his faculties to the realization of his country's ends. The movement at this point stops, in all the races of antiquity. With them the most comprehensive form of altruistic love was the love of their country. Only the Jews rose to the conception of a love of God ; and this was secondary to fear as a motive for obedience to His commandments. The last extension of the field of love was given by Christianity in its conception of the love of humanity; that is the communication of complete and uncontrolled liberty of thought and action to every living man. The aim of the love of humanity is the complete removal of all control and all law, and the establishment of universal unrestricted liberty. This, however, is only possible in conditions where life is not dependent upon law.

The ideal which was superseded was that of justice ; and abstract justice, as we have seen, is the principle of equality between two conflicting opposites. The conflicting opposites here are love and hatred ; and justice demands that every step in the growth on one side shall be accompanied by a corresponding increase on the other side.

Hence we find that, in history, intensity of love for what we approve of is counterbalanced by intensity of hatred for what we disapprove of. In earthly affairs the human judge is no party to the suit; he stands between the wrath of the avenger and the punishment of the culprit; his task is purely intellectual, that is, to equate the injury he inflicts with the injury which has been inflicted by the culprit. In his mind there is no room either for hatred or pity. With the Divine Judge the case is otherwise. He is the avenger of injuries against himself; and as no human intelligence can fathom the end against which those injuries are dealt, neither can it form any idea of the extent of the injury, or of the degree of severity which is appropriate to the transgression. No criticism of the Divine Justice is possible until we have a full comprehension of the Divine purpose against which we have offended, and that we neither have nor can have; but the whole of Scriptures, from Genesis to the Apocalypse, make it abundantly clear that His wrath is as infinite as His love: and this is the teaching of the Church. So far as it maintains control, and by a system of rewards and punishments restricts liberty, it is a continuation, in the Divine doctrines which constitute religion, of the ethical teachings of history.

The affection of hatred is seldom ascribed to God, even in the Old Testament. He hateth nothing that He hath made. The emotions that are most commonly attributed to Him in dealing with malefactors are wrath and indignation, which are indeed a sufficient antidote against the influence of universal love. 'The Lord thy God is a jealous God, and visiteth the sins of the fathers upon the children.' In the Christian doctrine of salvation by works the same attitude is maintained. But there can be no doubt that in the Jewish religion hatred against enemies is approved amongst men. It is the Royal Saint who exclaims 'perfecto odio oderam eos qui oderunt Te'. In our own day it is the most highly advanced nation in many of the leading characteristics of civilization which openly, and without a vestige of moral compunction, proclaimed the full righteousness of the principle of hatred, and in dealing with its enemies logically carried it out to its most hateful consequences in deceit and cruelty. We see, for it is in facts we are dealing with, that the uninstructed sense of duty does actually recognize here also the parallel growth of opposites, and asserts the equal value, to evolution, of love of friends and hatred of enemies. Even the most elevated morality stops short of branding hatred as always and absolutely bad. All it demands is that it should never be raised to an end in itself, that it should always be employed in the interests of love, and limited by what they require. Only when it goes beyond that point does hatred become hateful.

Whereas, then, the earliest form of our religion hesitates to attribute to the Deity the feeling of hatred for offenders, but substitutes in its place the severity of a righteous judge, the doctrine of salvation by faith, which is the peculiar and distinctive side of Christianity, frees itself wholly from the concepts of Law and justice, and puts in their place love, as the sole guiding principle of all action, whether Divine or human. In their rules for the relations between man and man the Jewish and the Christian Churches differ. The first endorses as valid the principle of hatred to enemies. David is not reproved for his treatment of the Jebusites; Saul is rejected for his mercy to Agag: extermination is the reward of defeat. The Christian Church, in its doctrine of works, applies to human relations the feelings which the Jew ascribes to God. It is severe to offences, but views them as a Judge and not as a prosecutor. It hates the sin but not the sinner. Vengeance must be restrained by justice. And this, in human affairs, is a material advance. Hatred does not pause to calculate a proportion between the offence and the punishment; justice must.

Moreover, both in our religious and in our ethical values, the concept of Justice is no longer strict. It is very largely modified by sentiments which are closely akin to love, such as compassion and mercy, and especially forgiveness of sins, which is conditioned in the Divine Judge by a similar forgiveness on the part of the sinner of the offences of other men against himself. These relaxations of strict justice in favour of Divine and of human love occupy a higher place both in religious and in the ethical scales of value than justice itself. They were not unknown either to the Jewish prophet or to the philosopher in Greece, but they received their first clear statement in the Christian doctrine of salvation by faith, and it is to that they owe their great prominence in the doctrine of the Church and in the ethical thought of the laity. In dealing with an enemy we now have an ascent of three steps, hatred, justice, and mercy; and the highest of these is mercy.

The inculcation of love by our mothers in our early life makes it hard for us to recognize the value of hatred, but in the mediaeval Church it was recognized and probably exaggerated. With them religious rebellion justified torture, and though they stopped short of death they made over the infliction of the last penalty, in its most painful form, to the civil arm, a procedure which reflected no honour either on the clergy or on the laity. It is true that we must hate the sin and not the sinner, but the criminal owes no gratitude to the impartial judge who hangs him but does not hate him. Justice makes no call on the highest virtue; gratitude is the fruit of mercy, and mercy the fruit of love.

Purgatory

Another point for comparison is the following. When the Kingdom of Heaven has been imparted by grace to a man in this life, he is, unless he falls away from grace, secure. So long as he retains his faith, his salvation is certain; when he loses his faith, it is lost. Degrees of virtue are of no consequence when faith, and not virtue, unlocks the gates of heaven. And virtue, it must be remembered, is obedience to law, while sin is disobedience. When faith is the means of salvation a man is already, while on earth, in possession of heaven so long as he is in a state of grace. 'Theirs is the kingdom of Heaven.' There can be no intermediate condition. This doctrine, though it follows directly on a belief in salvation by faith, allows no room for salvation by works, and those whose disposition has been so completely transformed by grace as to be indifferent to all earthly interests must in every society be so few that the Church would be unable to discharge its task of keeping alive the Christian faith. It, in fact, pre-supposes the immediate arrival of the Kingdom of heaven, accompanied with the exclusion from it of that vast majority of mankind who have not been vouchsafed an almost impossible holiness. It postulates an immediate παρουσία, and takes back the Church to the days of the Apostles, when that was commonly expected. It was the delay of that event, and the necessity of keeping alive during the evolution of the moral code the belief of humanity in the unchangeable and eternal ideal of another state of existence, that compelled the Church on earth to accept morality. This it first adopted from the Jews, and it has continued to modify it, on the same principle as directed the Jews while they were a progressive race, by inspiration on the prophetic side of its compound nature. The growth of dogma on its moral side was absolutely necessary if the Church was to retain its hold on humanity and keep alive the promise of the Kingdom of Heaven.

Of all the supplementary dogmas by which the morality of the Church has been modified, it will be allowed that that of purgatory is one of the most important, and it agrees with secular morality, as indeed with all the Divine works on earth, in having two contradictory elements, one of which is good and conduces to growth, whereas the other is evil and conduces to decay. The good resides in the dogma of purgatory itself; the evil, in the means by which that dogma is applied. Without a full belief in the justice and mercy of God a religion must be one of fear, and all religions of fear are superstitious. They work for the degradation of mankind and not for its elevation. No man can honestly adore as a God of love a Being who condemns the vast majority of his creatures to endless torments for a failure to attain a perfection which had been denied to them from the beginning of time, and which may be dispensed by Him, at His own free will, to the very few whom He had elevated, irrespectively of their own virtues, at His sole unbiased choice. But the attribute of love could be maintained if He provided for all who were not wilfully alienated from Him a place after death where they are fully purged from their offences in this life. When we turn from the question of the actual existence of this state, intermediate between earth and heaven, to the rules under which it is administered, our first remark will be that the independent action of the human will does not continue in another world. That it does, cannot be asserted either by the philosopher or by the divine: by the first because, if he is consistent, he must admit that his knowledge is bounded by experience; by the divine because his concept of free will is borrowed from morality, and is transcended in another world by the dissolution of the union between good and evil, out of which all morality is derived. The gift of entry, the term and all the incidents of residence, must therefore be solely determined by the will of God. On all these points our only source of knowledge is the inspiration which has been accorded to the Church. The validity of that is not a question within the scope of philosophical criticism, its agreement or difference with the spirit of morality is a matter of very urgent concern of ethics, and it is the subject of this essay.

The means by which an appeal to God may be made on behalf of souls in purgatory are of two kinds, either by the prayers of their survivors, or by the exercise of their authority by the priests. Against the first of these morality has nothing to urge. On the contrary, it is in complete sympathy with it. Prayer for departed friends is in agreement with the most elevated emotions of love and purity, and it keeps alive the consciousness of the connexion between the moral rules on this world and their final end in another. The same agreement with morality cannot be asserted of the belief in the dispensation of purgatory by the authority of the priest. The assertion and exercise of that authority lost the Church of Rome the allegiance of half her subjects, and should its own contention be correct their schism has divided their souls from Christ.

Ethical Elements of Belief unstable

In comparing the theological with the ethical aspects of morality we may be allowed the following conjecture, namely, that if ordinary morality, in development, suffers change, so also must the belief of the Church so far as it gives direction to conduct. The whole duty of the earthly kingdom, which is the Israel of God, is to keep alive among men, until the destruction of the present earth by the arrival of the Kingdom of Heaven, the memory of the destined Kingdom, and of the great sacrifice by which it was purchased. In order to perform that duty it is clearly necessary that the Church's doctrine should not contradict the teachings of morality, whose place is to preserve life on earth and to promote the increase of life. That morality itself, like the process it directs, grows and suffers change is, I think, certain. The only permanent unchanging principle is that of justice, or the ratio of equality between conflicting qualities, the equality not being exact, but subject to slight deflections, comparable in some respects to the surds in the common ratios of arithmetic. So long as the deflections from strict equality are on the side of life, and are not excessive, life will certainly advance; even excesses above the exact half in the principle of law may be of use to correct a previous excess of liberty.

Every complete system of ethics which adopts as its final end some consummation of action within this world contradicts, as has been shown, both science and ethics. Science deals with law and not with life, and the inquiries of ethics reveal nothing but a continuous growth without an end. When the final end is placed beyond the sphere of morality, it becomes a question in what way the practical rules of morality are to be connected with it so as to form a single system. Ethical beliefs develop with the general growth of a nation. Where the ethics are stationary, so also is the civilization. In Israel, where no distinction has been drawn between the voice of duty and the voice of God, the growth was marked and it was purely religious in form. The advance in meaning between the uncompleted sacrifice of Isaac and the consummated sacrifice on Calvary was incalculably great. But the course of evolution was not arrested by the latter. What that achieved was the Kingdom of Heaven, not to be introduced on earth until some unknown period, and after the total extinction of the present dispensation. In the meantime the human race must continue to develop. Its growth in civilization will be conditioned by a growth in its secular morality, and unless there is a corresponding growth in the moral dogmas of the Church, the two will cease to correspond; the latter will be left behind by the former. Either the dogmas of the Church must develop, or the Church itself must become the enemy of life and light; and those are the sole ends for the promotion of which it owes its existence.

The development, however, will not affect the dogma of the deposit, which it is the duty of the Church to hand down unchanged from generation to generation until it shall be realized at the last day—that is, the promise of a life exempt from bonds of all kinds to all who have retained their faith to the end. Change must be confined to those dogmas, inherited from the Jewish Church, which prescribe the rules for human action in the meantime. In the Christian Church there are many, but the more important of them are those which regulate the strength and the intimacy of the control which is to be exercised by the priest over the layman in the daily relations of life, such, for instance, as the dogmas which refer to confession, purgatory, and the remission of sins. These may all be developed to a point which completely extinguishes the liberty of the individual, and without so much individual liberty as constitutes freedom there can be no free State and no national development. The freedom of the individual lies in his voluntary obedience to his conscience, and when, for his conscience, he substitutes any external authority, even if it be that of the Church, he ceases to be a free man. A race of men who are not free cannot exist. They must eventually perish, and with them the secret of the Divine promise. Finally, obedience to the conscience is submission to the law which is the necessary means to increase of life.

Not only, in all societies which are in a process of growth, must the dogma of the Church on earth, as distinguished from the Kingdom of Heaven, undergo change and development in proportion to the changes of its moral feelings, but the changes must certainly vary, in substance and in direction, to accommodate the variety of national ideals in the conflict between which the development of life depends. Thus the moral teaching of the Church in a nation whose leading instincts are commercial will not be identical with that in a nation where they are military. But the main determinant in the differentiation of the moral codes of the Church is derived from the relative proportions between the two elements of law and liberty which are found in the various national ideals of freedom. These two elements may, and actually do, vary in almost any proportion between the total exclusion of law, which is anarchy, and the total exclusion of liberty, which is slavery. Any composition of the two in which liberty is the final end, and law the means, is freedom, though it may be moving in the direction of either anarchy or slavery.

Power of the Church varies directly with Influence of Law in Politics

In all Christian nations the final end is the Kingdom of Heaven, that is, liberty in another life. It follows that the earthly institution whose task it is to keep alive this ideal must maintain the elements of liberty in the first place in a pair of opposites, and only admits law so far as it is necessary to the maintenance and growth of liberty. To what degree that necessity extends, and by what limits the influence of law must be defined, is a question that has never been answered or even seriously discussed. The true relations between liberty and freedom have indeed never occurred to philosophers; and, even were they recognized in the abstract, their practical application is of great difficulty. It will, for example, readily be admitted that at the present day, in England, the proportion of liberty to law is largely in excess of equality; that the excess is so great as to be a threat to freedom cannot be asserted with the same confidence, though it is quite possible. Anyhow, the proportions vary, and it is a rough general rule that in those countries where the value of obedience to the law stands highest, and the people are most ready to submit to it, the moral influence of the earthly Kingdom of God will be greatest, and its power over the actions of daily life widest and most penetrating; whereas in countries where the spirit of liberty is stronger than the spirit of law the moral influence of the Church will be slight, and the religion of the people will centre round the doctrines of the Kingdom of Heaven.

Ritual

The moral power of the Church may be safely tested by the variety and elaboration of its ritual. Where ritual forms a prominent part in a religion the influence of the clergy over the daily life of a people is great; where it does not, it is weak. Ritual arises out of the conviction that the nature of the deity differs so greatly from the nature of his worshipper that communication between the two is only possible through the mediation of certain rites or ceremonies. It was almost always added that the power to perform those rites was confined to certain men or classes of men, who had gained it either by instruction, or by heredity, or by some other definite means of communication. Some belief of the kind stands as the foundation of all religious institutions. Without the attribution of a Divine qualification which distinguishes the minister from the layman, it is hard to see how a Church can retain any power for long. The priests would be like judges who had no authority from the State whose law they administered. In its more primitive forms religion consists almost exclusively of ritual, or the formal rules, which render possible communication with the deity.

The practical moral aim of ritual is so to affect the mind of the worshipper as to make it susceptible to the emotions on which the creed is based. If the creed is one of terror, and the deity is represented as hostile to men and rejoicing in their sufferings, it will be calculated to inspire terror: if as all-knowing, all-powerful, and perfectly just, awe and reverence. The emotions excited by the idea of the deity will at the same time be transferred to the mediator, and will always be some shade of fear or awe, according to the character which is attributed to the object of worship. The final end of ritual is reverence and not love. From the medicine man to the Brahman, no minister seeks to conciliate the love of their clients, but all insist most strongly on their respect. The reason is that ritual is itself law, and a check on life, which, if pressed too far, may extinguish it; and respect is the emotion which goes with law, whereas love is the emotion of life.

In the same way as the judge requires and gains

honour as the representative of the State, so does the priest as the representative of the Divine Ruler; and his honour and power will be proportionate to the strength of the spirit of law, and in inverse proportion to the spirit of life, in the race for whom he officiates as intermediary in Divine ceremonies. In this respect, reverence for ritual and tolerance of moral development are directly opposed. Where ritual is powerful there will be little growth in morals or none; where moral growth is unchecked, ritual will be disused. The nation is most fortunate which is able to retain the respect of law and the love of life in due proportions, giving a slight lead to the love of life. Russia is a country where, since its domination by the Golden Horde, political and social growth has been suspended. The same absence of change has been reflected in the moral dogmas of the State Church; they have had no history. At the same time the ritual has attained an unsurpassed splendour. The dogmas of the Latin Church have reflected in their gradual development the civil developments of the Latin race. In Spain, where the growth of freedom has been the slowest, the power of the Church has been the highest, her dogma the least affected by change, and the largest proportion of her total income has been spent on ritual. In England, where the simultaneous growth of both law and liberty, that is to say, of freedom, has been steadiest, the conservatism of her State Church has been balanced by the liberalism of her dissent. That this fundamental distinction is no obstacle to their combining on questions where the national moral ideal has been plainly at stake is frequently shown by the union of the establishment with dissent when both are threatened by a foreign enemy. The religious parties have, in this respect, reflected the behaviour of the political parties in Parliament.

Ritual is a characteristic of the Kingdom on earth. To that stamp of Christian whose attention is confined to the Kingdom of Heaven, and whose aim it is to realize that at once, and without waiting for the second coming of our Lord, every form of ritual and all fixed liturgies are an abomination. He represents a complete rejection of authority, which corresponds to nihilism in politics, and which cannot survive among people who are living together in conditions of co-operation. At the other end are they who, caring little for liberty, magnify the power and the splendour of the clergy in such a way as to make the Church despotic in all things, down to the most insignificant transactions of life. And not only the relations between the clergy and the laity, but all other subjects of belief which are concerned with the Church on earth, are (I am merely stating a plain fact) liable to great variations.

Within the Roman Church itself even the forms for celebrating the Mass are not *de fide*, or everywhere, or in all ages, identical : among Christians of other denominations the differences are enormous. The doctrines regarding confession, penitence, and absolution have undergone radical changes during the history of the Church, and have diverged in the opposite directions of the despotic power of the Church and the complete independence of the layman. Similar differences have arisen regarding excommunication; the causes by which it is justified, the methods of reconciliation, and the authority by which it may be inflicted—the supreme bishop, or the whole body of believers. Other forms of belief may be mentioned, such as the existence of angels, and the intercession of saints, which take a part either of supreme prominence or of almost complete neglect, according to the dispositions and the previous histories of the professing races.

Dogma which is above Evolution

One part of the religion has remained practically unchanged. That is the Baptismal confession, which summarizes those doctrines which in all places and at all ages constitute the Christian Faith. This is the message which it is the duty of the Church to keep alive. All its separate parts are equally essential to salvation. No man can question any single doctrine, such as the Divine Fatherhood, the Virgin birth, or the resurrection of the body, and remain a member of the Universal Church. Nor is there any earthly authority which can dispense with or modify any one of those beliefs. The whole is eternal and unchangeable. And the final end of the belief is ethical. It is a new birth, the creation of a Christian disposition.

The division between the eternal doctrine and the varying rules of conduct was established very early in the History of the Church, and was completed by the final crystallization of the Baptismal profession, which, in its primitive form, had been in use in the times of the apostles, and had been modified in such a way as finally to exclude the Pantheistic tendencies of Greek philosophy, which, unless they were defeated, threatened to convert a Jewish religion into a Hellenic mysticism. This measure has been deplored as fatal to the future prospects of Christianity; but, in the first place, it saved it from degeneration into an obscure school of ascetics, which, even if it had lasted so long, would not have withstood the shock of external invasions, and in the second place would have continually diverged from and fallen behind the advancing current of public morality.

The rules both of ritual and of conduct generally belong to the legal side of our religion, and are a survival, in a modified form, from the law of the

DOGMA WHICH IS ABOVE EVOLUTION 275

Jews. The original modification, which was indeed a radical change, was brought about by the preaching of our Lord, and by the prophetic inspiration at the Pentecost and during the early years of the Church. The rules for the Kingdom of Heaven are the immutable deposit in the charge of the Church on earth. They are above morality and exempt from growth. This is not the case with the rules which govern the relations between the clergy and the laity. They are for daily application of a morality which is continually growing under the influence of the spirit of life. If the Church were to exclude the Heavenly Spirit from operation on its practical side by the attribution to its practical regulations of the same fixity which undoubtedly belongs to the symbols of its faith, it would cut off from itself every connexion with life. It would give a complete and final victory to the principle of law, and abandon its sacred position as the guardian of life and freedom. The unity of the Catholic Church has, in fact, always been limited to the identical faith in the universal doctrines of the Kingdom of Heaven. Except for the comparatively short period when the Bishopric of Rome reflected the universality of the Empire, a period when there was neither nationality nor progress on the political side of life, there has never been any approach to unity in the Kingdom of earth; and the rise in the nationalities of modern Europe necessarily involved the multiplication of the Churches, all bearing the same message. The spirit of prophecy, had there been no Reformation, would be as nearly extinguished as it was in the Jewish Church between its final codification at the period of the captivity and the appearance of our Lord.

In order to maintain its hold on conditions of progressive civilization, the moral rules of the Church must be capable of modification in sympathy with the spirit of progression, that is, of freedom. But, on the other hand, their general direction must remain the same, and they must not depart from the final end of complete liberty after death. They must accept love and freedom as the leading principles in conduct, and new converts must transfer their spiritual allegiance from the priests of their old to those of their new faith. Only in that way can they become members of the Catholic Church, or Christ's Kingdom on earth. The attempts to realize in full the complete Kingdom of Heaven would extinguish at once every vestige of morality at whatever stage of development it might be made, from the lowest barbarism to the highest civilization; and, in order to retain its life, the morality of the Church must correspond with the morality of the layman on all points on which the ends or the means are not in vital conflict with its own. It was impossible for the Church to come to terms with the Circus, where the end was pleasure and the means cruelty; but quite possible in the case of the village festivals, where the means might be purified, and the end be transferred from a pantheistic to a supernatural form of worship.

Which of the rules of the Church belong to the Kingdom of earth and are subject to modification, and which to the Kingdom of Heaven and are eternal and immutable, is a question on which there is no approach to unanimity. That it has largely escaped the attention of the Church is, I think, certainly due to the influence of Greek philosophy, to the substitution of the metaphysical theories of reality of Plato and others in the place of the religious theory of St. Paul, and the search of the immutable within the world of experience instead of beyond it. By failing to distinguish, in its conception of the World, between the supersensible and the supernatural, it applies the term spiritual to both indifferently, and sees no incongruity in setting up as an object of worship an intellectual abstraction like the ideal of goodness, in the place of what must be the fruit of faith, an extra-worldly but personal God. The actual constitution of the World is such as to forbid the discovery within it of any single guiding principle, and in its pursuit of unity philosophy is compelled to empty it of all its contents. The absolute gives no guidance in conduct and cannot be made an object of worship. It silences both morality and religion. It serves no practical purpose, and it is a *reductio ad absurdum* of its own premises.

No one can doubt that the Church of to-day differs widely from the Church of the apostolic age. It is impossible to present even a rough contrast between any one of the innumerable forms of existing Christianity and the religion of the primitive Church, but in all of them the original creed of the Apostles, which was defined in the period before the Church had finally freed herself from gnosticism, remains the same. The only theological difference, excepting a slight modification in the definition of the Trinity which even Roman Catholics regard as not vital, is a doubt as to the sense in which the term 'Holy Catholic Church' is to be accepted. That this includes all who believe in all other dogmas of the same confession, and excludes all who, like the Marcionites and the Gnostics, differ from it on material points within the same creed, should be doubted by no one. But neither in that, nor in the further definition of dogma at Nice, is any reference made to the earthly constitution of the Church. Not even Episcopacy is asserted as an article of the Universal faith.

Growth, nevertheless, has proceeded in all

questions relating to the Church, or earthly Kingdom of Christ. It has been described and explained and defended in an eloquent volume by Cardinal Newman. Its most important step was taken only a few years ago, when, by the declaration of the infallibility of the Pope, the long evolution of its political form was concluded in an unlimited autocracy on an elective and democratic basis. But this form, which, in its main outlines, resembles that of the Roman Empire, is not by any means universal. It has not been adopted either in Russia, or in England, or by Lutherans, or by Calvinists, or by any other of the less important divisions; who all accept without discussion the whole of the apostolic profession of faith. Again, we may be surprised that neither of our creeds contains any reference to the Sacraments. The most sacred of all of them was instituted by our Lord himself at the solemn meeting which preceded His Sacrifice, and it is unquestionably as much incumbent on all the faithful as a belief in any of the dogmas of the Creed. But when we remember the expressed purpose for which it was commanded, our wonder ceases. It was to keep alive the memory of Christ on earth until His next coming. In order to do this, it was essential that the doctrines which interpret the rite should be alive, and susceptible of growth. Otherwise, if they had been substantial and real, or immutable, they would sooner or later come into conflict with the demands of the conscience, which grow and vary with the course of evolution. In that case we should be faced with the following dilemma. Either the conscience would prevail and the religion would be forgotten, or the religion would prevail and growth would cease. And if growth, or active life, were to cease, religion would contradict its own final end, which is the maintenance of life through law on this earth, as a preparation for life without law in Heaven. There was some reason in the boast of the Moravians that for them the celebration of the Last Supper was superfluous. If they had indeed attained the Kingdom of God in Heaven it was certainly true, but the accounts we have of them suggest that their goodness fell short of perfection. Anyhow, they did not withdraw themselves from worldly affairs, and all men who are so engaged must, if they would be Christians, believe in the 'Holy Catholic Church'—further, the rules of the Church for conduct on earth must be in harmony with the commandments of morality, or its mission will be unfulfilled. It is only in the next world that the Catholic Church can dispense with the law of morality, for there, there can be no growth; all will be either perfectly good or perfectly bad. There is no imperfection either in Heaven or in Hell.

Christianity a 'complectio oppositorum'

It is no new saying that Christianity is a *complectio oppositorum*. The fact is obvious, and here we have an explanation, and a line by which we can distinguish between the opposite classes of idea by which it is inspired. It has to provide for two opposite kinds of life, that is to say, for the life on earth which is the means to glory, and the life in Heaven which is its fruition. The means on earth is growth. This could not be otherwise; for the choice on earth is between progress and decay, and to select decay would mean eventual extinction. And growth can only be maintained for long by obedience to a well-directed conscience. A well-directed conscience will pay equal regard in its rules for life to law and to life. It is in fact law itself, and is the basis, and should be the pattern, of all political law. In this sense it comes that law, or the conscience, is on earth the root and the sole means of growth. In Heaven, on the contrary, where life is already perfect, no further growth is conceivable, and it is not desired; the function of law has disappeared. Men have then reached a stage which is completely raised above morality; for obedience has been replaced by love, and where love is perfect there is no longer any need for law, or threats of punishment. But perfect love not only excludes law and offence; it also destroys all life on earth; the attempt to realize it is nihilism.

It follows that the rules of Christianity must, and actually do, point in two directly opposite directions. Those relating to the Kingdom of Heaven are animated with a principle of conduct which, if universally adopted on earth, would be fatal to growth and the evolution of life. That would quite certainly be the result of the introduction on earth of the love and liberty of Heaven. As the parable tells us, until the coming of the last judgement the tares and the wheat must be allowed to grow together. We are now in that stage. For us on earth no last judgement, whether universal or individual, has yet arrived. In the meantime our moral duty is to promote development; and with that end the religious morality of the Kingdom of Earth fully concurs. Its final end is not to destroy growth and morality but to promote them. The Lord of the harvest does not stint His cultivation for fear that He may thereby benefit the tares as well as the wheat; He suffers both to grow together, until the last day. He commends the unjust steward, and His gift to the world is not peace, but a sword.

It is not, however, every kind of law that will serve the purpose of a continued growth. Men are forbidden to worship the image of anything in the

Heaven above, or in the earth beneath, or in the waters under the earth. All ideals that are placed within the limits of experience are idolatrous and in the course of a few generations must lead to destruction. Neither glory, nor pleasure, of an earthly type, may be set up as the final end of action, still less, the baser passions of lust and cruelty; and with them are condemned all the images of earthly power and beauty. They, and all images of the same kind, are forms of Pantheism, and they are destroyed by our Saviour by His teaching and by His death upon the Cross. And the last thing to be destroyed is Death, or the Law of the Conscience, that all things may be subdued under life or perfect Liberty. But, in the meantime, law must be preserved, not as an end in itself but as a means to increased life. Thus, while we are within this life, we are subject to an unceasing conflict between the rules of morality which preserve and promote life and the ideal of life which is above rule, that is, between a life by works and a life by faith. If we reject our morality we lose our life on earth, if we part with our ideal in another world we misdirect our conscience, and, again, we lose our life on earth. Our continuance of life on earth depends with equal necessity on the maintenance of two opposed beliefs, the doctrine of a life in another world without works and of a life within this world through work. But these, if rightly understood, are not contradictory. One stands to the other in the relation of means to end.

There is in fact no danger that the rules of religion will conflict with the direction of morality, if they fix the final end in another world; and it is equally certain that there will be such a conflict if the final end is either placed within this world or, as with the pleasures of the senses, adopted from this world. The pursuit of pleasure vitiates the aim of Islam; in the same way, the final end of power was represented in Chiliasm, a Jewish aim which was for a time attached to Christianity, but has now dropped away from it. Pleasure and power are the two main objects of earthly ambition, and, even when their attainment is postponed to after Death, their acceptance by religion gives them the first place in the moral conflict between opposites—one or the other of them becomes the supreme final end or *summum bonum*. And that position neither is qualified to hold. Each of them leads to results which contradict the aims of the conscience, and, by destroying freedom, puts an end to growth.

Expansion of Circle of Moral Obligations

The desires are centred on earthly ends, on pleasure or on glory; but, if morality is to be our guide, it is certain that the value of these counts for little or nothing, and that both must be postponed without hesitation to the commands of the conscience. In the ancient world the highest aim of the conscience of each man was the life of his country, and to that end he was required to postpone all the aims of personal desires. Since the advent of Christianity the circle has been widened, and the national community is called on to put even its own freedom to the risk in defence of the Kingdom of God on earth. And it submits to this danger, not from any disrespect for freedom, but from a firm conviction that only in this way can its own freedom be preserved, and that without freedom nothing else in this world is worth having. Patriotism represents the supremacy of national law; the Kingdom of God calls for the subordination of national laws to the Divine Law, which is for all mankind. But, while it subordinates, it does not destroy or abrogate; on the contrary, it confirms. In the same way as the private duty of the individual is not impaired by the addition of new duties to the State, so the political duty to the State will not be impaired by the universal duties of the Kingdom of God on earth. This was the view which was taken by the Catholic Christianity of the Middle Ages; which inspired its greatest Popes and united the princes of Europe in a league against Islam. In our own days the same idea appears in the moral guise of a League of Nations, who are to be united by the common end of the defence of the freedom of all against the overwhelming power of any one of them. This measure may be indispensably necessary, in the interests of the whole race, for the survival of any form of freedom, and consequently of progress. It will call for submission to a higher international law; but it need not weaken the hold of nationality.

We see that the tendencies of the Church and of the modern political conscience are in the same direction. The political conscience of antiquity raised the limits of morality from the individual to the smaller groups of the tribe or of the city, and beyond them to the larger dominion of the State. But there they stopped. The predominant morality of the whole Roman Empire was the morality of Rome. The universal empire of the Church, by substituting for earthly ends an end which was beyond the earth, made it possible to combine all the various conflicting moral ends in subordination to a superior Divine end. At the end of the Renaissance the national ideals and national morality resumed the leading position which they had enjoyed in antiquity; but in the meantime they had been thoroughly imbued with the tendencies of Christianity. The supreme final end of action was raised, at least in the more progressive nations, from the level of national law and freedom to that of a complete supernatural liberty, and a love of all mankind was superimposed on, without abrogating, the love of country. The Christian no longer goes to war with the end of suppressing the freedom of his enemies. His object is rather to maintain their freedom and to hinder them when they attempt to suppress the freedom of their neighbours. In the meantime, the reduction of the size of our globe by improved communications combined with improved means for the destruction of life—in fact, the whole advance of science in the production of force—has so greatly increased the difficulties in the maintenance of life that it is doubtful whether freedom will survive anywhere unless new means are developed for its protection. The empire of lawless force can only be met by a fresh extension of law, and the precarious and uncertain advantages which are secured by temporary leagues between nations must give way to a permanent international law, complete with its executive, and with sufficient sanctions for its observance.

This no doubt implies a very considerable increase in the restraints and the burdens which are imposed by law on humanity; but it is only by the acceptance of similar conditions that freedom has increased in the past or can be advanced in the future. The freedom of the individual is secured by his obedience to the law of his own conscience; the freedom of the nation by the obedience of its citizens to the national law; and the freedom of a group of Nations by the obedience of each one of them to the international law to which it has subscribed. And the conditional interdependence operates with equal force in the reverse direction. International freedom can only exist in a league whose members are free nations, and the freedom of a nation is conditioned by the moral freedom of all its citizens. The additional levels of law, in imposing new duties, do not diminish the area of freedom which had been attained on the old level. On the contrary they enormously extend it. They are the indispensable conditions of all growth. The life of the desert is called free, because there is no restraint. Neither is there any choice of activities; for that a man must go to London. It may be that only by submitting to the restraints of international law he can complete his conquest of the air. To the man who believes in the Divine government of the world, the simultaneous discovery of the art of flying and the proposal for a wide extension of law may not appear to be fortuitous. The new source of strength is still in its infancy, and there may be other inventions to come. The time may be at hand when life will find its conditions so much changed as to make it insupportable in times of war. How can the danger be averted ? Can human reason foresee the solution ? Will international law preserve us from slavery or extinction ?

It may be expected that the innate tendency of human desires will incline mankind to welcome the promised services to liberty, which are to be rendered by international law, and at the same time to ignore the additional burdens which it must impose. Men will represent to themselves that the end for which they submit to the new fetters is peace, which is the object of their desires, and not freedom, which is the proper end of their moral aspirations. This is not of necessity a cause for alarm, for in ordinary minds the higher order of aims frequently advances under the cover of the lower, and people who are fighting for freedom may persuade themselves that they are fighting for material wealth. Few can see more than one side of a question. But the two ends, though they may be confused, cannot be identified. They may frequently conflict, and the poverty of Switzerland in any sound judgement is immensely preferable to the wealth and the splendour of

Imperial Russia. The final end of international law is to secure the freedom of all the peoples on the earth. When that has been secured, there may no longer be any need for war. But it will not secure that the evil of war is not replaced by the much greater evil of slavery, or some other curse of the nature of which we can form at present no exact conception. That is indeed inevitable. The only unattainable end is the destruction of evil on this earth. Here we must be satisfied with the maintenance of growth through law.

We find then that the final end of liberty has to compete, first, with its own opposite in the complex which makes up the whole concept of freedom, that is, with law; and, secondly, with the various external ends of the passions such as power and peace and material wealth, which conflict with conscience and are inconsistent with further growth of life. A religion like that of the Hebrews, which identified the law of the conscience with the voice of God, was the apotheosis of law; that of the Gentiles made Gods of the passions, and their philosophy was tied to the earth. The complete triumph of force in the Roman Empire had secured peace, and deserved the gratitude of its subjects; but it had barred all further prospects of growth in civilization. The final end of the empire was law; and it remained the same until the Bishop of Rome succeeded to the power of the Emperor, and exercised it under the new final end of a perfect liberty in Heaven, which could only be attained by freedom on earth. The struggle between the two ideals of law and liberty was the severest the world has ever seen; it is still continued, and philosophy unaided has no certain means for predicting the issue. It will not, however, withhold its unhesitating approval to a scheme which seeks to advance the growth of freedom through a growth and extension of Law.

As a purely ethical reformation, the conscious raising of the final end of action for all mankind from earth to Heaven, and its transfer from law to liberty, is by far the most important the world has ever seen; and the most difficult. It can only be brought about through the production of a new disposition: a mind that is naturally turned to God. The Christian is holy, but free: the beatitudes are not commandments, but a description of the spontaneous reactions of his will; and that is what it is because he is the son of God, and in full harmony with His will—he is no longer bound, but already, so far as he is the son of God, at perfect liberty: and his soul will be filled with love and wisdom. The universal value of Christian dogma is as a means to the production and maintenance of Christian character, that is, of freedom on earth, leading to liberty in Heaven. Fear God and keep

His commandments ; this, says the Preacher, is the whole duty of man. ' Thou shalt love thy God with all thy soul, and thy neighbour as thyself ; this is the whole of the law and the prophets ' ; is our Lord's injunction. The two are incompatible ; for perfect love casts out fear. But Christianity maintains both ; one for the Kingdom on earth, the other for the Kingdom in Heaven. The new order implies a change of direction away from Earth to beyond the grave, and a revolution in the moral values.

It would be wrong to leave this subject here, with its prophecies unqualified, remembering, as we must, that the future, in evolution, never exactly answers to the past, and that the universality of change within the world we know necessarily falsifies, sooner or later, all rational deductions. The range of science may be extended, but its certainty will be reduced in proportion to the elevation of the stage of life with which it is dealing. It is more probable that the sun will rise a hundred years hence than that we shall be here : advance a thousand years farther ; our knowledge of the sun is practically the same, of ourselves we are wholly ignorant whether we shall still exist. Change in ourselves is brought about by changes in our environment to which we must either conform or perish, and of those the most abrupt and the most trying are those which proceed from our own discoveries and inventions! We have apparently accommodated ourselves to explosives and steam; of electricity it would be too early to speak; of the possible effects of flying or of radium we know next to nothing. Aviation might make dwelling above ground impossible; the great extension of subterranean labour might call forth a race of slaves. Who will be so rash as to predict what would be the result of the discovery of an unlimited supply of radium in any country, or of any other of the myriad secrets which nature still withholds? Many men of science have professed the hope that by perfecting the means of destruction they may make war impossible. To this no categoric answer is possible, and the best-founded conjectures are unlikely to be realized. All we can say is that man may himself succeed where nature hitherto has failed, and extinguish humanity on earth. Every rise in the form of an organism adds a new danger to its life. If it accommodates itself by abandoning war, it will enter on a new phase of evolution. How the dangers of a perpetual peace will then be provided for, we have no means of knowing. Nor have we the least shadow of a reason to anticipate that the new means which will be substituted for war will be any less to our taste than war itself, or, on the other hand, any more objectionable to our successors who must submit to them.

LIBERTY

FINAL ENDS

PHILOSOPHIC AND RELIGIOUS

LIBERTY

FINAL ENDS

PHILOSOPHIC AND RELIGIOUS

We have described the Ethical Law as the law of morality, when that has been supplemented by, and is guided in the direction of, a religious final end.

It was added that when the moral law is directed towards an earthly final end, the system is really philosophic and not religious. To this point I return. Its further explanation is the task of the pages that follow.

The Final End of Pragmatism

The most recent school of philosophy to attract a widespread and serious interest is that which, under the name of Pragmatism, has been preached in America by Professor W. James, and in England by Dr. Schiller and others. This distinction it deserves, not only by the originality of its thought, and the wit and lucidity of its exposition, but also by the still more decisive merit that it constitutes a real step in advance—one of the very few that have been made in thought since Kant's discovery of the Categoric imperative. Stated briefly, that theory is that the truth of a proposition and its value are identical terms, and that the value of a proposition depends on how it works. In other words, the sole test of truth is efficiency. The value of this theory is that it emancipates thought from the tyranny of the past and turns its head in a new direction. It transfers the centre of interest from causes to results, from the past to the future, from real or permanent existence to purpose or final end. The main problem of philosophy is no longer ontology or the discovery of the universal category of existence, but teleology or the discovery of a universal end of action; metaphysics must yield the leading place to ethics. The home of the new philosophy is in America, a country which has little or no past, and whose interest is centred on the future.

Efficiency, however, cannot be accepted as an end in itself, but only as a means to the attainment of an end which is good in itself. Iago was eminently efficient, and at the same time eminently bad. He was bad not because he was inefficient but because his action was directed towards a wrong end. The same thing applies to our judgements on all classes of conduct. Napoleon was the most efficient man in modern history, but no one would dream of calling him good: that he is not even acclaimed a

THE FINAL END OF PRAGMATISM

hero is due to a change in the final end of the modern conscience. This is the case with all our judgements on action. The criterion is always the same. It is not efficiency, either personal or communicated—for no man ever contributed more to the growth of society than Napoleon did—but conformity to an ethical ideal. Of the absurdity of a system of teleology without an ethical final end for the distinction between good and evil, the Pragmatist is fully aware; but, perhaps because he is dazzled by the greatness of the formal revolution, and partly, perhaps, because he is unwilling to break entirely with the system in which he was brought up, he devotes less attention to this part of the subject than it deserves, and elects, under the name of 'humanism', the satisfaction of human desires as the universal aim of conduct. To make their meaning clear, they depose Plato, but elevate Protagoras and the sophists to the vacant throne of philosophy. To the deposition of Plato we have no serious objection. From the time of Origen, and earlier, he has been in league with Christian thought, but his influence has always been perversive. Protagoras is radically incompatible, and his occupation of the vacant seat is like the irruption of the seven other devils in the parable. The last state of the victim is undoubtedly worse than the first. The correct determination of the universal final end is a matter of the highest importance; it is not easy, and it is not within the reach of metaphysics. The weakness of metaphysics lies in the fact that all things flow and no man dips twice into the same stream. The future, however near, never exactly reproduces the present; at a great distance the divergence becomes incalculable.

Final End external to Conscience

It is almost always held that if a man obeys his conscience he acts rightly. There can be no greater error. All that can be said safely is that when he obeys his conscience he does his duty. Provided that his conscience is in harmony with any considerable body of ethical feeling, so much may be admitted; but it does not at all follow that because he does his duty he does what is right. A General may be impelled by his conscience to divulge secrets which he has learned in his official capacity; or a fanatic to murder a brave and intelligent King. An interesting case is that of Timoleon, who killed his brother whom he loved because he made himself tyrant of Corinth. Grote, the historian, condemns the act on the ground that the moral tie which binds a man to his country is not so strong as that which binds him to his family; but this view would be rejected not only by all virtuous pagans, but by the great majority of virtuous Christians. The literary judgements on Brutus, who killed his benefactor Caesar, have been equally conflicting. To Addison he is a hero; Dante puts him in the lowest depths of Hell, and between the teeth of Lucifer.

The verdict in each case would be ruled, not by the conscience of the individual concerned, for that, in all, commanded the action, but by the reasonable belief. The general acted rightly if the conscience of the individual has no regard for the interests of the State of which he is the servant. Ravaillac was justified, as indeed was the massacre of St. Bartholomew's day, if the secular interests of the Church take the precedence of those of the nation, and of the ordinary moral law which forbids murder; Timoleon, if, as most of us hold, the wider interests of his country came before the narrower interests of his family; Brutus, if the interests of a party are to be preferred, not only to friendship, but to the wider interests of the State. If relative value is to be determined by the width of the interest, and not by its intensity in the mind of the individual, the aim of the Christian martyr who died for a universal liberty, which is not of this world but common to all men, stands certainly highest. So much, I think, must be conceded; but, of all conceivable ends, the prospect of complete liberty in this world kindles the intensest flame in the minds of the multitude; and this nevertheless, as is shown by history, leads to death. What is required in order that right action should be coincident with duty is that the conscience should be properly directed. The effect of early education on the conscience is incalculably great, and may direct it to nearly any end. The Spartan mother bred the Spartan soldier; the Christian mother, the soldier of the Cross. A scheme of education which shall secure peace by making the children incapable of resenting any injury is probably feasible; but it is open to the objections that it would, in the first place, make those who accepted it the slaves of the more warlike races; and afterwards that it would indirectly corrupt the warriors themselves by an undue success. What, then, is the practical use of an organ like the conscience, if, by early education, it may be directed to the approval of almost any conceivable act, however nefarious? The answer is plain; the conscience is not to blame: what perverts it to bad uses is the rational aim by which it is directed.

Varieties of Final End

We must now pass in review some of the principal final ends which have, in fact, been offered and accepted for the guidance of human conflict, universally, and as a whole. The importance of the question is recognized by Pascal when he writes (*Pensées*, xv. 7), 'La dernière fin est ce que donne le nom aux choses. Tout ce qui empêche d'y arriver est appelé ennemi. . . . Ainsi, le mot d'ennemi dépendant de la dernière fin, les justes entendaient par là leurs passions, et les charnels entendaient les Babyloniens.' Nearly all great wars have had their origin in a difference, more or less clearly understood, between the respective final ends of the conflicting nations; and not between the moralities themselves, except so far as they have been modified by the final ends.

The Commands of Morality Disconnected and Categoric

By morality I mean the mass of disconnected maxims which are based on the reactions of the conscience, and the distinction between the dough of morality and the leaven of reason lies at the basis of all moral speculation. The dough, and by that is meant the whole of moral reactions regarded as one body, the Corpus of moral judgements, is as like and as unlike in its appearances in various races as their various physical forms and constitutions. It is easy to distinguish the outward forms of a German and a Frenchman, a Chinese and a Negro, but the points in which they agree are far more numerous than those in which they differ. So it is with moralities. Some observers are so much impressed by their similarity in type as to declare them eternal and immutable; others, of a sceptical turn, make the most of their differences in detail. As we find them, they are large collections of contradictory principles, which work in all directions, and with no internal steadiness of action. There is no developed system (or rather Corpus) of morality which does not contain within itself all the leading principles, at least in germ, which are to be found in all the others. For example: Thou shalt do no murder; thou shalt not commit adultery; thou shalt not steal; thou shalt not give false witness, are universal maxims for the guidance of conduct; but they are not connected by any common end. No morality contains within itself a universal final end by which relative values may be determined. The conscience, and on that they all depend, rejects calculations, and has, certainly, no conscious purpose.

The moral legislation gives no final end. It is absolutely categorical, and gives no reason for its commands. This is plain, and calls for no proof. But it is interesting to remark how it comes about. The aim of morality is to preserve life, to promote growth, and to prevent death and decay—beyond that it does not go. Its supreme final end is the final end of growth, or of evolution, and that is the province of the intellect and not of the conscience. If the intellect asserts that it has demonstrated what is the final end of growth, that would, necessarily, be the final end of activity. But it does not follow that it would be the end of the conscience. It would only be that if the rules which were deduced from the intellectual final end were in agreement with the rules which were enacted by the conscience. If they differed, in ever so small a degree, the intellect and the conscience would be, to that extent, in conflict. If the difference were at all material, it would be necessary to choose one or the other; that is, either our intellect or our conscience, for the practical guidance of our activity, that is, of our life. If we reject the conscience, we must at the same time reject all the moral values which are based on it. It is therefore a matter of the highest importance to compare the practical working of the final ends which have been proposed by philosophers with the practical working of the rules of morality. If we find that they are materially discordant, and elect to abide by our intellect, we at the same time reject the moral values, and condemn as useless all systems that may be based upon them. This will be our intellectual belief; and our conscience, though it will not be annihilated, will be perverted. The result will be that the attempt to rationalize the conscience, or to systematize it by providing it with a final end, will be to divert it from its real final end; and thereby greatly to reduce its strength, and in extreme cases entirely to silence it.

An illustration will perhaps help us to understand. The greatest master of ethical thought has propounded as the fundamental axiom of the science of Morality the maxim that man must always be regarded as an end in himself, and never as a means. His disciples have deduced from this maxim the legitimate conclusion that the criminal law is opposed to morality. It is certainly not opposed to the common moral sense. In this case then scientific morality contradicts current morality. Philosophers admit this, and they claim that current morality should be reformed by education. As a result they promise in a distant future an era of perfect happiness on earth. This then is their final end: perfect happiness on earth. It is true that their interest in the 'scientific' section of their proof is so absorbing that they keep the connexion with the final end in the background, and hardly attempt to establish it. But this, it may be submitted, is a mistake. Men of a practical mind do not care to discard the principles on which their prosperity has been hitherto secured, in favour of one which is new and untried, on the bare assertion of the inventor that the change will make them rich beyond the dreams of avarice. They have been assured the same thing of other principles by other inventors, and recognize the bait. With regard to the theory that all men are absolutely equal and free, as ends in themselves, it may be urged that however true and valuable that may be, it is equally true and perhaps more important to evolution, that all men are born unequal; and that the interests of all must be limited by the interests of each. There are few, moreover, whose natural conscience does not tell them that when a man is proved to be unfit for his freedom, he forfeits it. That is, ultimately, when the primitive freedom of one clashes with the primitive freedom of another, and the conscience asserts the primitive right of self-defence. Up till lately the question has rarely been complicated by religious considerations. Now, an attempt is made to enlist the support of Christianity to the doctrine of human perfectability in this life. The object of these pages is to show that the attainment of perfection is asserted by Christianity to be possible, but only to those who are included in the Church; and to them in another life, and as the fruit of concentrated effort in this life: whereas to those who are not within the Church there is no salvation.

Eternal Values can only exist beyond the reach of Law

The intellectual completion of morality is the discovery of an end to growth which will not contradict the moral rules; and the result of our previous discussion is to show that the discovery is impossible. Growth, on the whole, is conditioned by the parallel growth of opposites, and if any one of these opposites be selected as the final end of action it will cease. Where no final end of growth can be discovered there can be no final end to offer to morality; and a final end to human action must be found elsewhere, apart from and above morality. But so long as the earth endures, men must act, and, unless they are to disappear, they must obey the rules of morality. We therefore get two sets of values: the changing values of life on earth, and the eternal values of life in heaven; the values of a life which is ruled by law, and of a life which is above law.

Earthly ends, Glory or Pleasure

Final ends may be divided into two main classes in accordance to their being located either in this world or in another. When located in this world they are the subjects of philosophy; when in another, of religion. Of the worldly ends the two with which we are best acquainted are, when appraised by the rules of morality, not ends of action at all, but rewards for certain classes of act which may or may not meet with the approval of those rules. The ends to which I refer are, first, glory, and, secondly, pleasure. It would be idle to assert that every act that brings glory; still idler, that every act that brings pleasure, is commended by the conscience. We will give the precedence to the end of glory, which serves as the basis of the military spirit; and then take the end of pleasure, which is the end of commerce. Both ends agree that the world is on the whole good, and that human perfection may be found within this life, if anywhere.

Glory

The desire of glory, or distinction, is probably as common as the desire of pleasure, but, as it is opposed to pleasure and can rarely be prosecuted except at some expense to the individual, as well as for another reason which we shall soon come to, it is less popular, and has received less attention than it deserves from our popular and strongly hedonist philosophers. It is, however, at least equally important to the student of liberty, and in some ways more respectable. Whatever form it may take, the universal aim of the love of glory is the production of power, or of the reputation of possessing it. It may at first be thought that as the production of power is the only criterion we have of advance in civilization, this aim is in direct agreement with progress; and this no doubt explains the glory, or admiration, which is the reward of every great achievement; but it will be found that the direct pursuit of glory does not, in the end, promote progress, and that it is in direct opposition to the common rules of morality.

The motive pervades every rank in society from the lowest upwards. The objects of pursuit are honour, power, social standing, reputation, and the like. To the ambitious, riches are never valued except as a means to one of these. Pleasure to them is not only unsought as an end, but is often sacrificed and always despised. Desire for glory scorns delights and lives laborious days, and for that reason has been truly described as the last infirmity of noble minds. It is the sole motive employed in schools and universities for the stimulation of effort, whether in the class-room or on the cricket-field. The same motive explains the humbler ambitions of the tradesman to stand well with his fellows, of the lady to win admiration by the costliness of her apparel, and the almost universal passion for social success. It inspires the conqueror in the field and the artist in his studio, and its influence is clearly attested by men of science, in the warmth with which they dispute questions of priority of invention or discovery. Finally, of all earthly qualities it is the one which is most frequently and most properly attributed to the saints in heaven, where it is reflected from the Glory of God. In our devotions, what we give thanks for is our hope, not of pleasure or happiness, but of glory.

Its part in daily life is not without claims to moral respect. In Germany *Selbstgefühl* is a term which appeals very clearly to the approval of the conscience. Its literal English translation, self-consciousness, has not the same connotation, and its place is taken by the somewhat similar but not identical feelings of self-respect, or personal dignity. All are forms of self-assertion which are more akin to the military than to the commercial spirit. They are clogs to the pursuit of pleasure, but wings to glory. They are all incompatible with the proper spirit of Christianity, which is humility and self-effacement. In a democracy, where the leading aim is pleasure, the value of self-respect is liable to be overlooked; but, though it might not secure in the judges either strength of character or learning, it would at any rate save them from being buffoons.

A motive which is so widely spread in its working,

so closely in agreement with the growth of civilization, so rich in its rewards, and so elevated in its attributions, might surely be accepted at once as the universal end of right conduct. And it has been, and still is, widely accepted as such. It was the leading principle of the Roman Empire, and it has again been raised to that rank by an influential school of thought in Germany. But it is in direct opposition both to Christianity and to Christian morality, and, if they are to take the lead, glory on earth must be rejected as the supreme final end. One aspect of the supreme final end in Christianity is glory in Heaven, and that is to be gained by the sacrifice of glory on earth.

An objection which is fatal to it is that liberty and glory are wrongly connected. The strong and the distinguished are always inferior in number to the weak, and when their power is unrestrained it tends to be concentrated in the hands of one person. This means the extinction of all liberty except that of the Prince. Such a condition is common. It is not necessarily opposed to happiness, if the ordinary liberties of domestic life are left untouched; and it is consistent with the greatest power in international relations; but so long as it is maintained in law and in Politics, it is a fatal bar to progress; and progress is the sole criterion of morality. The last phase is slavery for all, and an irresponsible tyrant; who may be removed by Palace intrigue, but is succeeded by another with the same power over his subjects. The tyrant himself, who is raised above both law and public opinion, is still the slave of his desires, and his own liberty is usually a curse to him. The fundamental objection to glory as an earthly end is that it is opposed to justice. The sole concern of glory is with the qualities of men and their comparative merits. For the liberties of the multitude it has no regard at all. Its leading principle is competition, and, when it needs co-operation, it is always in the service of competition. In Christian morality the liberties of the multitude and co-operation take the first place; merit and competition the second, and though still necessary, a subordinate place.

In all intermediate stages of growth, liberty for the strongest is only demanded as a means to their domination over the weaker, of the few over the many. Liberty as thus understood is not the leading principle, but domination over others and the glory of the few. The restraint of law is removed, and, with it, the restraint of morality, and nothing is put in their place. We have a return to the primitive anarchy. When, on the other hand, the multitudes call for law it is solely as a means to their own liberties, which cannot be maintained at all except at the cost of a reasonable restraint on the liberty, or activities, of the few. When the restraint on the few becomes stricter than is required for the preservation of a reasonable amount of liberty to the many, it becomes excessive. Perfect liberty can be the portion neither of the few nor of the many, nor can the distribution of liberty be nearly equal over a whole community without endangering its further growth. The task of law is twofold: first, to secure to every man his share; secondly, to see that the distribution should roughly conform to merit.

It is certain that to take glory as the supreme final end of action will not permanently advance the life of humanity; and that, unless contradicted in time, it will lead, eventually, to the complete cessation of growth. Yet it was the aim of the great mind of Plato, and is retained by the eugenic philosophers of our own time. The scientific objection is that it is impossible to breed an all-round excellence, and that, while fixing the attention on certain good qualities, you necessarily disturb the right balance on which strength of character depends. The ethical objection is that it is unjust, and that, in advancing the growth of the eminent, you must overlook the claims of the multitude. The objection of injustice applies with equal force to the erection of the other reward, that is, pleasure, to the position of supreme final end. But in that case the weight is thrown into the opposite side of the scale. It is the multitude that profit at the expense of the eminent. The eventual result is the same, the ruin of both.

Pleasure

Pleasure is a reward of activity, and its pursuit might be expected to encourage activity. This is as true as it is of the pursuit of the other reward, that is, glory, but like that, as a final end of conduct, it contradicts morality, and eventually puts an end to growth, though its operation is different. In the early days of a nation's life, while the force of evolution is young and uncalculating, the spirit of growth will concentrate the aspirations of its citizens on the highest developments of life, and the kinds of activity by which it will secure its pleasures will be the most elevated. It will devote itself to literature, science, philosophy, and the fine arts, not because the pleasures which are derived from them are in themselves superior, but because those forms of activity are most in accordance with its own temperament. Pleasure indeed is no test of conduct; its intensity or quality, or whatever makes it desirable, is always dependent on the conformity of the activity from which it is derived with the disposition of the actor. The pleasures of the Bishop are not those of the burglar, but it is impossible to prove the intrinsic superiority of either over the other.

This implies no condemnation of pleasure in itself. The proper function of pleasure is not to guide action but to reinforce it in its efforts against restraint. Without the prospect of pleasure we should have had neither great art, nor science, nor literature. Lacedaemon deliberately sacrificed pleasure to the prospects of glory; and, though there is good reason to believe that she was as richly endowed with natural gifts as any branch from the Grecian stock, the legislation of Lycurgus at once put an end to her growth in any direction but that of war. She contributed nothing to the civilization of the world, and she used her excellence in arms to arrest the growth of the neighbouring civilization of Athens. The love of glory and the love of pleasure are both necessary ingredients in growth, but, when taken as final ends, they are opposite and mutually destructive. With a great artist the love of his art will come first, and it will be reinforced by the prospect of the most elevated type of pleasure. If either glory or pleasure is the end, the act becomes theatrical, and the art petty: both are popular and commonplace.

All variations in value are fundamentally moral, and are based on the nature of the activity and not on any difference in the reward itself. This in the case of glory is obvious. However greatly a man may be delighted by the consideration which is derived from his wearing a fine coat, the highest form of glory is only gained by victory in a great battle, or by a work of genius. It is the same thing with pleasures. The difference between a common and an elevated pleasure lies not in the pleasure itself but in the activity which calls it forth. It is irrelevant to inquire whether the pleasure of the common man in a good feast or in third-class music, or the pleasure derived by his intellectual superior from hearing a symphony by Beethoven, is the greater in quality. Each prefers his own, and the question will never be solved. This is not the case with the activities. The common man will not say that he prefers a street song because it is more elevated, but because it gives him pleasure, whereas a symphony only bores him; and he is at liberty to choose what pleases him best. It is indeed a matter of experience that correctness of judgement depends as much on education as on natural taste, and that the rare appreciation of the noblest qualities in art is largely derived from a familiarity with the objects in which they are exhibited. I have heard one lady admit that Raphael had a considerable talent for decoration, and another that Titian did not appeal to her; and both were women of a high class of proved artistic genius, but of limited acquaintance with foreign art. Mr. Ruskin had only a slight appreciation of Michael Angelo.

As soon as pleasure is recognized as the supreme end of conduct, this claim is unanswerable. If there is no other end of higher value, each man must be right in choosing his own pleasure. But it is clear that the moral law does not make pleasure its final end. We have seen that that has no final end, and pleasure, when it is put forward for that position, it rejects with scorn. The motive of Ulysses was domestic faithfulness, and that nerved him to despise the attractions of Calypso and the Sirens; but it was not a universal end. It was supreme against pleasure, but it gave no reason for its supremacy, and was not consciously deduced from any known end of universal obligation. If pleasure had been the supreme end, he would probably have preferred an immortality of delights with the goddess. At any rate he must have debated the question; but his heart was firmly set on his duty. To set up pleasure as the final end of conduct is to supersede the moral law.

In every collection of human beings the undistinguished are of necessity far more numerous than the distinguished. As soon as it is recognized that each man's pleasure is the right standard for his own guidance, each man will be justified in seeking his own. Criminal pleasures will be barred, partly by the remains of conscience, and partly by the consideration that they interfere with the pleasures of others; but the consistent hedonist will assert that even the most immoral, if they are free from the second objection, should be exempt from criticism and from penalty. The purveyors of innocent pleasures, authors, artists, showmen, newspapers, and others, must suit their wares to their market, and as the public is undistinguished they must be adapted to common tastes. Elevation whether in style or in substance will daily be less aimed at, and will finally disappear. We shall gradually conform to the lower orders of life, like the sailors on the island of Circe.

A further objection to pleasure as a recognized end of conduct is its strong tendency to individualism. It will not be asserted that pleasure can be felt except by individuals. A collective body can no more be pleased than it can eat and drink. In this respect it differs from glory. A nation may enjoy a high name irrespective to the reputation of particular citizens. 'Civis Romanus sum.' This explains why patriotism is high in the esteem of a nation whose leading aim is honour, and not in esteem when the leading aim is pleasure. A Roman poet,[1] writing at the height of the Republic's glory, gives the first place to his country,

[1] Lucilius. Mommsen, *History of Rome*, iii. 463.

and the last to himself—'Commoda praeterea patriae sibi prima putare; Deinde parentum; tertia iam postremaque nostra.' The English banker, writing at the height of England's commercial prosperity, places, as we have seen, the claims of the family before those of the State, and has little doubt as to the concurrence of his readers. Any one whose memory carries back more than a few years must recollect that patriotism was then held in low respect by many of his more cultivated friends. Its place of honour among ourselves has, in part at least, been restored by the war.

The brutalizing influence of pleasure as an end is clearer when money comes to be regarded as its equivalent. Judas carried the purse, and holy men in the East still refuse the contact of the accursed thing. Where pleasure is regarded as the end of life, money, though still condemned by the higher order of minds, will surely be accepted as its equivalent by the great and daily increasing preponderance of the common or baser multitudes, whether of the rich or of the poor. But while the higher orders of pleasure, such as those which are derived from the fine arts, may be infinitely distributed, and may rise in value the more they are shared, this is not true of money itself. No two men can share a shilling without dividing it, and the value of sixpence is only half that of a shilling. The pursuit of money thus tends directly to disruption. Contrary interests, even in money, are not to be condemned in themselves; but, unless the competition is held in check by some higher end which is common to both the rivals, they must inevitably end in the extinction of co-operation, and the substitution of hatred for love as the dominating principle in the relations between man and man. The result is the same as in the competition for glory and power; but with competition for pleasure, or money, it takes on a more extreme and uncompromising form. The pursuit of power, in its higher developments, admits of co-operation and self-sacrifice and love, within the limits of the country; the pursuit of money admits of no co-operation higher than that of trading societies, and it would be idle to assert that it encourages love and self-sacrifice among constituent members of those. The explanation is that glory can be divided without being diminished, whereas money cannot. The humblest soldier reflects something of the glory of his victorious general, and, in reflecting, enhances it; the factory hand gains nothing from the wealth of his employer, nor can he, without diminishing it.

Science has no power to prophesy

We might examine many other solutions of the problem, but the result would always be the same, and always must be so long as the methods are philosophical, and the data and the final end within the province of philosophy, that is to say, within the limits of our experience. Whatever final end on earth is proposed, the pursuit of it must inevitably lead us to destruction. The reason is not far to seek. We are living under conditions of growth ; the mere fact that we desire a final end at all is itself a symptom and a condition of growth ; without growth we should have no moral values, and a system of ethics would be inconceivable. It would no more enter into our heads than it does into the brains of bees or ants or of any other of the lower products of life, whose growth, if any, is imperceptible. But nature does not disclose her end. If men conjecture an end, and attempt to support it by argument, the whole action is merely an incident within growth, and cannot possibly be the real end. The only result is to support one member in a pair of opposites, which is useful as long as the contest is maintained, and destructive as soon as its opposite is worsted. The end of science will always be the object of its desires, that is, either pleasure or glory; and those are not incidents in growth but rewards for success, without the penalties which always attend it. Progress without drawbacks has never been seen on earth, nor does Christianity promise it there.

As it is impossible to ascertain the end of creation, it follows of necessity that any end that is set up within creation must contradict the real end. No power of divination, not even a universal knowledge of all facts within his possible experience, would have enabled the lemur to foresee Plato ; nor can we either accept Plato as an end of our development, or draw a picture of anything higher. The assertion that an exact and complete knowledge of one moment would enable us to reconstruct the whole of the past, and predict the whole of the future, ignores growth. It may be true for the past, but it would not enable us to predict with complete accuracy a single moment in the immediate future ; and the part which was wanting would be all that was of value to the ethical philosopher ; it would be the record of a future growth. The whole of the present world-experiences is the sum of additions which have not been minute or microscopic, but infinitesimal, and which are therefore irreducible to number and useless to science. What science deals with are the single impressions which are made on our senses, and growth leaves none.

Growth is always spontaneous

Another advantage which a supernatural has over any natural end is that it is appropriate to all stages of civilization alike. For a natural end to work, or have any influence on conduct, it is necessary that it should be conceived as being attainable, or at any rate that it may be more nearly approached, in this world. How far that expectation is justified in fact we have already seen. A brief success is invariably followed by a reaction which carries society farther back than the point at which it exchanged the promptings of conscience for the guidance of a conscious end. But that is not the point with which we are now concerned. When a society sets up a worldly end, it must necessarily conceive that end as a kind of definite standard, and the standard must derive its shape and its colouring from the experience and the aspirations of the people by whom it is constructed: it will be wholly unappreciated and inapplicable to a people whose experience and aspirations are not the same, and to them, like an ill-fitting suit of clothes, it will be an encumbrance. No scheme of civilization, however elevated, will serve for the education of a savage. His growth must be from within, and spontaneous. Education may fire the ambition, but it can never provide the pattern. A change of pattern by itself is not growth, but, if imposed by a conqueror, however benevolent his intention may be, an incident in decay.

To take political institutions as our field of illustration. The proper end of all political thought is freedom. Its object should be to devise laws and institutions which shall give the widest possible scope to liberty, that is to say, to the spontaneous growth of the whole society in all directions. The type of institution which best meets this need varies greatly with the character of the citizens, with the internal stage of growth of each society, and with the external dangers with which its independence may be threatened. In some States a personal autocracy may be the best suited for the purpose, and, so long, as the autocrat remains amenable to the public opinion of the citizens, this may, in serving growth, be a true form of freedom. But when that condition is not fulfilled, when the autocrat is not in sympathy with the aims of the citizens, it is no longer freedom, but tyranny. An autocrat who extends his rule over an alien people is necessarily out of sympathy with his subjects, and his rule is the worst form of tyranny, or the complete abnegation of liberty. The rule of Alexander in Macedonia was freedom : in Greece and in Asia it was tyranny.

At the other end of the scale we have a government by the whole mass of the people expressing its views through its representatives. That this has been successful in England is due, ultimately, to the intensely conservative temperament of the English people, which while demanding personal independence for each individual has always recognized the superiority of merit, and has been willing to submit to its guidance in all matters which do not affect their personal independence. The object of every Government is twofold. First, to preserve, to the State which it represents, its independence, or freedom from domination by aliens; and, secondly, to preserve the freedom of each class within the nation from the domination of other classes. No nation is really free, or able to maintain its independence against foreign aggression, unless every individual within it who has not forfeited it by crime has his own share of liberty. That share may vary in amount, but the least which is consonant with freedom is a complete equality before the law. Every member of a representative Government is then representative in two senses of the word. In the first and most important sense, he represents the whole nation as opposed to other nations; in the second sense, he represents the particular class or interest by which he is returned. With respect to the first aim, a member of the Commons stands on exactly the same footing as a member of the Lords or the King; and, as the unity and the strength of the whole nation are inextricably bound up with the freedom of every one of the classes of which it is composed, each representative of the State should be as solicitous for the freedom of all as he is for his own.

This, however, is impossible. Not only is human nature as prone to selfish as it is to unselfish motives, but the life or growth of all communities demands a struggle between classes. In a caste system, or with socialism where class conflict has been eliminated, there can be no growth. The representation of each separate important interest within a country is necessary, both to counteract the selfish influence of other classes and to ensure that the needs of every class should be known and considered.

Of the two characters of a member of the House of Commons, that is to say, the representative of his country and representative of his constituency, the former is by far the more important, and it really embraces the latter; for in an ideal Government each member will recognize that the interest of his own constituency is really identical with that of all the others. The aim of all will be the same, and the function of separate representation will be merely the provision of complete information in regard to the several interests which are to be coordinated by legislation. Men whose aim is the greatness and freedom of all must rise above the ordinary level of their constituents, and must be independent of them. Ultimately, they must be judges rather than suitors, the élite and not merely the elected. On the other hand, as representative of his own constituency, his part is that of a barrister whose duty is to represent their special interests as completely and as persuasively as he can. Unless he combines both characters, his representation will be imperfect, and his government will fail. If he is only a Judge with the greatness of his country as his sole aim, he will be unaffected by the strife of interests which is the essential feature in the growth of his nation, and in striving for greatness he will sacrifice growth: if he is a mere advocate, the assembly to which he belongs will lose the common end which binds them together, and will degenerate into a battle-place for minor, discordant aims. It is necessary to freedom under any government by representation that there should be both the general, common end of patriotism and the special, conflicting ends of particular interests; and that, of the two, the former should take the lead.

True representative government is only possible under conditions which are the result of a peculiar national temperament and a long and favourable historic growth. Where those conditions do not exist, the attempt to impose it is sure to fail. In a country, for instance, where patriotism is bound up with religion, and the bulk of the population is broken up between two widely different and irreconcilable religions, there could be no common aim to unite the national assembly. It would be divided into two groups between which no composition was possible, and, as the decision must always rest with the majority, the minority must always lose. No member could pass from one side of the House to another, and there could be no change in the relative strength of the two parties. The result would be a tyranny of the most odious type for the minority, from which they must revolt; and the nation would be plunged into civil war.

The minority would seek the assistance of their co-religionists on the other side of the frontier; and that would indeed be offered. The peccant majority, if they had no foreign co-religionists to appeal to, must yield and becomes the slaves of the minority. The representative assembly will cease to exist. It is useless to draw out all the possible consequences should the majority itself succeed in procuring foreign assistance. The whole world might be involved in war.

We may proceed to consider the position of the member, as representative not of his country but of his constituency. We will imagine that the population has been distributed into various interests (without that, indeed, no large population could exist and maintain a common life) but that those interests did not conflict. This might be attained by a division into hereditary castes, where each man was contented with the manner of life to which he had been called by Providence at his birth, and had no dream that he could fill another better, or desire to attempt it. Add to this that the appreciation of money and of luxury was incomparably lower than it is with us; and wealth was almost exclusively valued as the means for a display which should confirm distinctions which had already been assigned by birth, and not for purposes of personal comfort. A fine diamond in such a society would be of value to a Prince, but of no value, even for the purposes of exchange, to a cobbler. This state of things may easily be established by an excessive application of the principle of heredity, and has been brought about by that means in India. It is of great value in giving stability to a society by eliminating the disruptive tendencies of competition; but in eliminating conflict it is deadly to growth and it is the hated antithesis to democracy; which, however, reaches the same end by a different road, that is, by excluding the influence of heredity. The uncontested domination of a single hereditary caste, whether they are priests, or landowners, or great

GROWTH IS ALWAYS SPONTANEOUS

merchants, is as fatal to liberty as a pure despotism is; but not more fatal than the domination of mere numbers.

In short, a representative assembly, in order to contribute to freedom, must combine two conflicting principles. In the first place it must be united by the common principle of patriotism; in the second place it must be divided by the conflicting tendencies of class. In a state of evolution neither of these principles is more essential than the other; both are indispensable to ordered change. Growth will not be introduced in a stagnant society by the introduction of any form of free institution; for they are all the product of growth and stages in the direction of further growth. The introduction of a democracy of representatives in India would be followed, not by peace and internal prosperity, but by war, both foreign and civil.

But it is nowhere possible to foresee the direction which growth will take; a wise statesmanship will be contented if it can remove the bonds which choke it. Of those, in India, the most powerful is the competition of British Trade; and the British Parliament may be the source from which it has most to dread.

Utopias

All fixed forms of policy, whether they have been selected or designed by the conscious reason, are Utopias. The American constitution was not of that class because it was not merely philosophic, but had a long period of previous growth in England, and within itself it contains a sufficient combination of the germs both of conservatism and of change to redeem it from finality. Plato's Republic was inspired by the principle which we have called glory. As an institution, it was meant to be final: it neither contemplated nor admitted change in its own forms. It was, so far, on the same footing as the Hindu caste system; it paralysed growth, and was directly exclusive of freedom. It might, like the Spartan State, have contained elements of stability, but it could never have promoted the all-round growth of its citizens. Even the military spirit, which was its special distinction, must have begun to decline as soon as it had attained a sufficient success.

Most of the Utopias of modern Europe have been based on the Christian principles of liberty, equality, and fraternity—that is to say, the abolishment of law, whether moral or political, the refusal of reward for merit, and the elimination of hatred in social relations. This is nothing else than the immediate establishment on earth of the Kingdom of Heaven; and of all perversions it is the most deadly—at any rate if judged by its immediate results. Those are the annihilation of the growth of past civilization and a return to the conditions of primitive barbarism. Whether life will return after destruction, and what the character of the new growth will be, are questions to which it is impossible to give a categorical answer.

LIBERTY

SUMMARY

LIBERTY

SUMMARY

Conclusion

In my first essay,[1] I concluded, on an abstract consideration of the principle of the parallel progression of opposites, that 'the universal criterion of value is approximation to an unknown end. And, as all evolution up to the present day has taken the form of the parallel progression of opposites, so long as the same process is maintained, it must be impossible to discover that end within the world of experience.' With this negative conclusion I stopped. The conclusion has now been confirmed, or illustrated, by an examination of a considerable number of instances in which men's activities have been directed towards worldly ends. And this leads to the positive conclusion that the final end of action must be placed in another world, beyond the range of experience. Morality can only be reduced to a system by the discovery of a universal final end, and, for that, it must be indebted to religion. No philosophy of Ethics can be completed, except with the

[1] *Ethical Aspects of Evolution*, p. 16.

assistance of religion. Ethics is the philosophy of morality, and a philosophy that contradicts morality has no right to that title. No final end that may be realized on earth, whether it has been designed by philosophy or been actually attained by conquest, will conform with the dictates of morality or serve the purposes of advancing growth or evolution or increase of life.

The decisive advantages of Christianity for the completion of an ethical system are two:

First, its universality.

Secondly, the complete consonance of its direction with that of the moral law.

Its universality makes it equally applicable at all stages of evolution. However highly a civilization may be developed, it is always at precisely the same level, when compared with perfect liberty, as it was when the movement forward commenced. The Nicobar Islanders may be taken as an example of the nearest approach to the perfect liberty which can be seen on earth. But if their activities are free, it is because they are so limited as hardly to rise above the level of the animals by which they are surrounded. Practically, the whole range of social activities is unknown to them. The consequence is that as soon as they come into contact with a more advanced people they die out. An extension of activity, or of liberty, is only purchased by an extension of law; and from that point of view, every advance in civilization appears to be a retreat from the perfection of the Heavenly liberty. This, however, it is not. The increase of life counterbalances the increase in law, and the total distance remains the same. Every advance in activity is paid for by an increase in law, and unless the price is paid, all the advantage, and much more, is lost. In worldly affairs, that is, in evolution, the distance from pure liberty is always the same, all gains to liberty being counterbalanced by an equal increase in control. It is true that the balance is never exact. If it were, progress would cease: but the slight deviations on either side do not affect the whole character of the process; and they can never be more than slight without reversing its upward direction. Pure liberty can only be attained where there is no evolution, and no civilization of the kind we know on earth. What are the conditions of a living soul when beyond this earth, philosophy neither knows nor can ascertain. On this earth law is as inevitable as death.

When a man is assured that where there is no death there is no law, his mind becomes fixed on the contemplation of liberty, and on the place where that is to be found. Earthly affairs cease to interest him. His efforts are divorced from the present, and are focussed on a life beyond the grave. He has no worldly aims or fears. This gives him a spirit of independence, and raises him above all worldly restraints, especially above the law of morality. Morality is based on justice, and justice demands an equal return for injuries. Where there is no morality there is no justice; and perfect life means perfect love, which like the rain from heaven falls on the just and the unjust alike. This lofty detachment raises him, as it does the Hindu ascetic, above all the worldly impediments; but unlike the ascetic, he is not only raised above justice but he is still attached to his fellow-men, without any distinction of race or sex or condition, in all the regions of the world, by the sacred bonds of love. The aim of love in this sense is to raise one's fellow to the same level as himself, above human needs, above law, and the possibility of sin. In this sense, and in this only, is the love of man the same thing as the love of God.

This love retains the spirit within the bounds of experience, and gives it an object which is higher than experience. It is the love of the apostle, and of the true missionary, which seeks to save but not to civilize.

A complete superiority of this kind constitutes the Kingdom of Heaven. It is not the common property of all men, and never will be. At the Last Judgement it will be granted to the elect only. Our Saviour thanks His Father for having conceded it as a boon to His own personal friends. The Church recognizes it in her saints. But, in the meanwhile, until the Advent of the Last Judgement, the government of the world must be carried on, and the principle of Government is the Law. This, for the Jews, was the law of Moses, as modified, in time, by the spirit of prophecy. The Jews drew no distinction between revelation and conscience, or between law and morality. Their principle of government might be described as the law of morality as described by Moses and the prophets. But the purpose of the law of morality is confined to the world of experience. It has no final end of which we can form any conception. It cannot serve as its own end, for the realization of law only means the extinction of life, and leaves law nothing to act on. Nor can the end be life only, for life on earth without law is inconceivable. The law of morality has no final end but the continuance of an endless progression of both the conflicting opposites of life and control.

In accepting the law of morality for the guidance of her relations with the earth, the Church recognized that, at the time of its instauration, morality was wrongly directed towards the realization of worldly ends, and that the pursuit of any of those ends inevitably led to the loss of liberty. Whether the end was commerce, or conquest, or law, or liberty, or knowledge, or any other earthly achievement, success always meant death. Civilization was everywhere threatened with extinction in all countries except those of the east; and there, where no positive end was recognized, it had already lost the power of further development. Of this truth Judea itself was a striking example. Prophecy had ceased, and society was closely enmeshed in the net of priestly glosses on an ancient law. The darkness, both there and elsewhere, was at once dispersed by the proclamation of the liberty of the Kingdom of God as the final end, and the marshalling of all the forces of morality under the supreme command of love for the prosecution of that end.

The task, then, of the Church was twofold. First to keep alive on earth the memory of the great sacrifice, and of the instauration thereby of the new ideal of life. This memory was perpetuated, and renewed from generation to generation, by the men whose lives were devoted to the glory of their Saviour, and whose deaths were like His—by the confessors and the martyrs of the Church. The second, and not less important, portion of the task was to keep alive the people to whom the promise was made, and to deliver them from the bonds by which their growth was stifled. This could only be accomplished by the regulation of their morality, and by directing their actions in such a way that the growth of law and of liberty should be about equal, and that neither should overwhelm the other. The supreme end of Christianity is liberty, but not liberty in this world; the aim of the Church in this world is freedom, or liberty conditioned by law.

No detailed account is required to show that Christian morality has made a long advance beyond all that preceded it both in liberty and in law. The first council at Jerusalem released Gentile converts from all restrictions of the law except those relating to meat which had been polluted by being offered to an idol, or by the manner of its death; and to sexual indulgence. The whole system of circumcision and temple offerings were swept away, together with all the minor observances of the Law. The tyranny of a priestly caste was broken, and the spiritual rulers were chosen from among the people themselves. On the other hand, the subject-matter of the law was enormously increased, and the means of enforcing it strengthened, until they culminated, in some regions of the faith, in an ecclesiastical tyranny which surpassed in severity all its predecessors. Thoughts and intentions were brought under the same condemnation as deeds; marriage was restricted in choice and, to a large section of the community, forbidden; the liberty of divorce was removed; offences of a kind which were formerly the object of ridicule were now erected into capital crimes; all conveniences and recreations, such as slavery and the gladiatorial games, which involved the degradation of others, were condemned; the slightest difference in religious faith was punished by torture and death. Add to all this the unrivalled effectiveness, as an instrument of domination, of the system of auricular confession, and of the redemption of souls from purgatory. All these developments of law have occurred within Christianity, and most, if not all, are peculiar to it. When they became insupportable, they led to the revolt of the Reformation. They were a deadly peril to Christianity as a whole: first, in turning the attention from the Kingdom on Earth to the Kingdom of Heaven and thereby disparaging morality, and finally by obscuring the Kingdom of Heaven and opening out the fatal mirage of a perfect liberty on earth.

Nevertheless, however greatly it may have exceeded from time to time on the side of the law, the supreme final end which has directed the morality of the Church on earth has always been liberty, and not law. It retained law, because to abandon that would be the same thing as to abandon morality, and morality is the safeguard of life upon earth; but it was impossible for it to forget that its mission on earth was so to preserve life as to make it fit to dispense with morality by rising above it. It was impossible for it to regard morality as an end in itself, or as anything better than a temporary expedient, which the saints could be better without even while on earth. But the rule of the saints and the abrogation everywhere of morality was never contemplated.

It was plainly foretold that life should be maintained on earth until the sudden appearance of the Last Judgement; and that at that time men would be found at their ordinary occupations. Till then, therefore, law must be retained.

There are, however, not two Churches, but the same Church with two aspects; one directed towards the attainment of liberty in Heaven, the other towards the maintenance of freedom on earth.

On the one hand, the Church proclaims the complete equality and autonomy of all men, and the infinite value of each individual soul, which brings it about that the loss of a single soul is incalculably greater than the loss of the whole universe of sense. Religion claims for its own province, as supernatural, everything that is above or exempt from phenomenal qualifications or natural law. Christianity defines as its God a Being who is neither single nor many, but Triune; and, as the real and permanent self in every man, his soul, clothed in a body which is neither material nor subject to decay. The soul is not subject to human or natural law, and after its sojourn on earth it may be lost or saved to all eternity. Being real, what the soul is we can neither define nor learn; it cannot have either beginning or end, for those are phenomenal predicates. Nor can there be either free will or natural law; there is nothing but the will of God. This is the doctrine of the Kingdom of Heaven.

The Kingdom of Heaven is gained by conformity with God's will during the life on earth. God's will is love; His state is unconditioned, and He is above law. That state it is impossible to realize on earth. On the contrary, experience teaches us that the only means to the maintenance and growth of life on earth are law and conflict. The inner guide to each man in this conflict is his own conscience, and with his conscience as his prompter he works out rules of conduct. But neither is the conscience itself, as we know it, supernatural, nor are its rules, nor are earthly good and evil. Only God is good, and without the Divine guidance no maxim or rule of the conscience is really good or permanent. The natural tendency of the conscience impels in the direction of an earthly end, such as pleasure and glory, or, in the province of the intellect, to abstract conceptions. All these lead nowhere. The Divine guidance manifests itself in a new birth, which transfers the end of action from this world to another, from the phenomenal to

CONCLUSION

the real. The guiding principle of the new creation is love, which is in conformity with the real nature of God; and its direction is perfect liberty for all.

The constitution, however, of the world is such that no phenomenal quality can subsist or grow without its opposite. Why this should be, or that it is actually the case, is a question of reality, and beyond the reach of the reason. Religion teaches it, and accounts for it by the myth of the Fall. By this principle it becomes impossible that life or liberty should subsist or grow on earth unless under the conditions of law. The most abstract definition we can give of life is change that is enduring and continuous. Both the duration in life and the continuance of change, which makes, impossible ever to step twice into the same stream are due to the interaction of law and life. This conception is useless to science, which deals with consequent facts and not with continuous change; and it is only when transferred to religion that it becomes mischievous. To the supernatural it is clearly inappropriate. The conception is abstracted from natural data of the senses, and does not go beyond them.

The Church, which is Christ's Kingdom on earth, has a double task set before it: first, to secure for each of its individual members his salvation in the next world; and, secondly, to maintain the life and growth of the human race in this world. For the second section of its task it has only the rules of morality to depend upon, but in order to render them appropriate to its purpose it must put them in the second place, and recognize that law generally has no value except as a means to life, and that no new law is justified except as a means to growth.

Ethical thought begins with morality, and, in its most abstract form, morality is a combination of law, or rules, with free will. What makes an act moral is responsibility. There is no merit in a forced obedience, or blame for an involuntary lapse. Liberty to obey or disobey was, as Dante says, the last and greatest gift which was given on his creation to man by God; and it is shared by no other form of life. Conformity with the Divine nature is made to consist in obedience to the Divine law on earth, that is, religious merit; and the reward is the admission to the Kingdom of perfect liberty in Heaven. All morality exists in this life, and nowhere else, and what distinguishes Christian morality from all others is that whereas the law, which is essential to the definition of morality, is placed in this world, its sanction, which is either above or below law, is placed in another. The sanction or final end of obedience to law in this life is a perfect liberty, or release from law in the next. The highest stage attainable in this life is freedom, or a continuous growth of liberty supported by a continuous growth of law. In Islam the supernatural reward, or final end of earthly action, is pleasure unmixed with pain. The reward of goodness is for that the greatest conceivable degree of pleasure.

The God of the Stoics was identified with inexorable law: the God of the Christians made law, and is in all respects superior to and unaffected by it. The only virtue of the Stoic was cheerful submission to an order which neither he nor God himself could modify: the Christian, during his life on earth, is endowed with a will that is above law, and his virtues consist in a free obedience to all the precepts of the Divine law, which is summed up in the single principle of love, love of God and love of your neighbour. The system of the Divine government of the world is resumed by antiquity in the Hindu doctrine of Karma. Reward necessarily follows virtue, and punishment vice. With the Christian there is no uniform sequence. The blackest sins are remitted on a change of nature which ensues immediately on faith; and faith is the free gift of God.

In the answers given to the problem of real existence we find the same fundamental contradiction. The Greeks, and all their modern representatives down to Spinoza and Hegel, accept without hesitation the postulate of uniform sequence as their guiding principle. This, Christianity directly contradicts. In the realm of real existence it is faith that prevails, not law. Faith as a grain of mustard will move mountains. The entrance of the Divinity on the life of man, and His departure from it, were miraculous, and its course a continued chain of miracles. The Roman Church, before declaring a man a saint, demands evidence of a miracle as the token of the Divine activity in his life.

It is impossible to doubt that in the Kingdom of Heaven, and that is the Christian term which corresponds to reality, law has no place at all. There is nothing but a perfect liberty, founded on faith and directed by love. But this has not yet been attained in the shifting conditions of earthly life, and while they continue it can never be. Indeed, to minds under the control of law a state of perfect liberty is not clearly conceivable.

All beliefs which concern the supernatural, or real, are received by faith, and are not the subject of knowledge. They may be accepted or rejected according to the natural temper or the education of the individual, or as God decrees; but they cannot be argued about, or, if they are, the argument is vicious and inconclusive. The Jewish beliefs that God is one and that He may not be worshipped under the image of any object of the senses are truths of this type. They are eternal and immutable, and though they may be added to, or explained, as in the Christian doctrines of the Trinity or the Virgin Birth, they can never be abrogated or become obsolete.

All experience, before it can be applied to action, must become knowledge, and in order to become knowledge it must submit to classification, that is, to law. A completely isolated experience cannot be either understood or acted on. No judgement which is derived from experience can be either exactly true or exempt from change. No two articles are exactly alike, but, in order to form classes, their differences must be disregarded. Again, the apparatus by which concepts are formed is never the same in two individuals, and the whole concept varies with the nature of the mind in which it is formed. The earth-worm has life, and must be credited with rudimentary concepts. But practically the whole of our experience is made up of what is known to us, but is not known to an earth-worm; and the mind of an angel may be as far removed from ours as ours is from that of an earth-worm, and still remain at an infinite distance from the unlimited mind of God.

The function of knowledge, or remembered experience, is, like that of digestion, but on a higher stage of evolution, the preservation of life. This task it performs by its influence on action. Action when influenced by knowledge through thought becomes purposive. But in man we observe a conflict of motives. Some motives we regard as good and others as bad. Both kinds may co-exist at the same time in the same mind, and they point to action in opposed directions; and then, before a man can act at all, he must choose between them, making up his mind to accept one of the two for his guide and reject the other.

A careful consideration of these two classes of motive compels us to conclude that the distinction between them is based on their opposite relations to the principle of evolution, or of growth. One class is in favour of further advance, the other is opposed to it. The first we call good, the second we call evil. The feelings with which we regard each of these processes respectively reflect the hatred that we feel for law, or restraint in itself, and the love we feel for liberty. The atmospheres may be compared with that of a small and stuffy room, and that of a mountain side, or of Land's End.

It would at first seem clear that the proper aim of action is the complete realization of liberty. But the complete realization of liberty is, in fact, nothing else but the complete abolition of law. The whole social structure, or civilization, which has been built on law, is then destroyed, and the bars which have hitherto pent up our most degraded impulses like wild animals in a cage are taken down. And it should be remembered that this is another and a far worse thing than a mere return to conditions of barbarism. Since that time the growth of the higher impulses has been attended by a corresponding growth of the lower. The cruelty of the revolutionist is far worse than the cruelty of the tiger, and his lust than that of the ape. The evils arising from the complete realization of law and the extinction of liberty are less likely to be disputed. The inevitable result is slavery. But this has not prevented the tendency from being set up as a ideal and exercising a most powerful influence on history. All dreams of universal empire have their roots in the desire to destroy the liberty of the subjects, whether they belong to the country of the aggressor or, still more obviously, to the country which is attacked. Slavery, again, is an evil which is practically unknown in the ranks of creation which are below man. A return to primitive conditions like those of the Nicobar Islands is not to be thought of.

Thus we find, first, that the complete opposition that exists between constraint and liberty affords an explanation of our distinction between good and evil. Regarded as purely abstract principles, liberty is good, and constraint evil. But in practice liberty is not attainable without constraint. Constraint when organized becomes law, and without law there can be no life. A good law is one that maintains and promotes the growth of life and liberty. So long as it performs that function it is the object, not indeed of love, but of respect and veneration. The conscience, whose place in the structure of the human mind is to influence action through free will in the direction of further advance, fails to discriminate between the devotion which is due to the unknown final end and the respect which all should feel for the recognized means, and lends to both an impartial support. So far then as our practical experience helps us, that is, within the limits of the knowledge which is the basis of all our reason, we have no means of ascertaining any single final end to conduct. Both law and liberty, as practical principles, are good when they are taken together, and each is bad when taken alone. If we consult our feelings, liberty attracts our love; law, our respect. Both are supported by our conscience. But it is impossible to make a single final end of both. Law and liberty are mutually exclusive.

In an essay on 'Justice' we discovered that justice was the property which rendered possible the development of all social and political relations. When we proceeded to define that property, we found that it is constituted not by one single principle but by the simultaneous growth of two opposed principles, those namely of equality and inequality. Any State in which all the citizens were equal in power or in property would be incapable of growth; and the same thing would be true of a State which excluded any considerable body of its residents from all share in power or property. Again, the same irreconcilable conflict was found between the impulses and the values which are proper to each principle respectively. All the labour which is spent on the higher forms of education, with a few scattered exceptions, is for the sake of distinction; and the reward is counted of higher value than a large income in money. When a nation goes to war, it usually is in order that it may be 'Über alles'. Success is admired, but it is usually gained at the expense of our neighbours. On the other hand, equality, as an ideal goal, has always appealed to the enthusiasm of the multitude. Liberty and equality are joined together as the watchword of progress; and religion teaches that all men are equal as the sons of God.

We are indeed justified in the belief that of the two opposite principles of equality and inequality which together make up justice, it is equality which has a right to the same position within its own pair as liberty holds in the pair of liberty and law. But it by no means follows that it must be the ideal or sole end of human conduct. There is nothing conscience tells us more clearly than that exceptional services ought to be paid an exceptional reward. In ordinary thought it is proportionate value rather than exact equality that would suggest itself as the definition of justice; and without a careful distribution of both punishment in proportion to offence, and of reward to merit, there can be no stable society. Neither can the total abolition of distinctions be made the sole aim of society, nor can competition be allowed to proceed unchecked. The conscience gives no certain verdict, or, more correctly, makes no universal choice. Its function is to indicate the path of advance, and it anticipates the process of further evolution. Like all natural growths, it is itself imperfect, and its anticipations, though usually, are not invariably correct. The moral judgement of the individual is binding on himself, but it need not be respected by the community to which he belongs.

When we proceed from the most abstract to the more concrete qualities, the case is clearer. Chastity is an exalted virtue with religion; morality approves of fidelity to the marriage vow; and neither will there be healthy growth without restraint, nor birth without indulgence. In the same way, peace is the greatest, except freedom and justice, of human blessings, but the conscience demands that war be chosen rather than those be sacrificed. Peace and perfect chastity are the ideals of conduct, but they are the religious and not the moral aims, and, however we may strive, they cannot commonly be realized till after death. The impossibility is absolute. Decay will certainly ensue on a peace that is unduly prolonged, and the reason gives way before excessive asceticism. Freedom and Justice are the highest moral qualities, but they are valued only on account of the liberty and love which they, as it were, hold in solution. They are not the pure ore; nor can that be won except in the Kingdom of Heaven. By no human effort can Paradise be regained on earth, and our religion does not promise it.

Many will be disposed to complain that this is unfair to the conscience, and that human nature generally suffers an injustice in being denied the power of rising on its own wings to eternal and immutable values. This complaint will not bear examination. The aim of the conscience is to foster beliefs which promote growth, and, at any rate so long as the whole movement is in that direction, the conscience will call those beliefs good, or of higher value in proportion to the degree in which they contribute to that aim. That there is any doubt on this point is due to the fact that there is one or more series of values for the desires, and another for the conscience.

The wise man of Greece, whose praise Lucretius celebrates, does indeed deserve the glory that is claimed for him and secured by the immortal verse. He set man free from the bonds of a debasing superstition. But what was the exact character of his achievement? So far as it had permanent value, it was a reform of method and not the introduction of a new final end. The final end of the religion of his own time, which he not unjustly brands as vile superstition, was to bend the forces of nature to the service of man. It had been handed down from the remotest antiquity, the chief step in its evolution having been the attribution to the natural forces of human shapes and passions, as Gods. This end Democritus retained: his aim was still the subjugation of nature. But the whole of the means of attaining it he swept away. The means were those which had been previously found effective in bending the wills of human agents to our purposes; and, before the formulation of the law of uniform sequence, no other method was even conceivable. But entreaties and propitiations, threats and deceit were all found equally ineffectual when addressed to inanimate objects, or to their supposed representatives as gods; and scientific investigation was put in their place.

This reform, however, valuable as it was in dealing with external nature, did not go beyond that. In dealing with other men it was useless, for the simple reason that in them we found free will, and the law of uniform sequence could not be applied. In what was by far the most important sphere of action, men continued therefore to make use of persuasion, or force, or fraud. In the meantime it became obvious that the employment of force or fraud in order to influence beings who were immeasurably our superiors, both in physical and intellectual power, was, at the best, a mistake. In religion they began to fall out of use, or to be employed only in cases where it seemed difficult to expect sympathy; and worship became more and more synonymous with devotion. The prevailing attitude toward their Gods of the men with whom Democritus was acquainted was fear, a humility which was degrading. The profession of ethical faith which antiquity itself regarded as its most elevated was that of the Stoic master:

But lead me, Jupiter, and thou dread Fate:
I follow cheerfully where you dictate,
Or, if being base, I flinch, I follow still.

There is no choice at all over the action, only over the temper with which it is acted.

A complete change in the relations between the human and the Divine was brought about by

Christianity. The Incarnation, and the taking of the Manhood into God, broke down the middle wall which separated them. Man became a partaker in the Divine nature, and, so long as he retained that share, it was not possible to regard him as a slave, still less a machine. The attitude of the perfect man towards his Maker is one of awe combined with a love that casts out fear : and the final end of every Christian is to attain this temper. This, however, is the lot of very few while they are on earth ; of those on whom it has been conferred by a special decree, and who carry about the Kingdom of Heaven within them. And the disposition that is involved in this is humility and selflessness. The only guide we have for discriminating between these is our conscience. The end of the conscience, however, is not the realization of any fixed ideal, but merely continued growth ; and, as growth is dependenton the existence in proper proportions of all the conflicting principles which make up life, it is not in the power of conscience to pronounce in favour of one in a pair of opposites and condemn the other, without defeating its own ends. It is not in its power to make an absolute classification of goods and evils.

A philosophical study of the conscience, which seeks to reduce all its commands to a common end beyond the mere survival and growth of the race, will not find that end within the circle of those commands. It must seek for it elsewhere. Finding no earthly end that will serve its purpose, philosophy will seek one in religion. The agreement or contradiction between the commands of the conscience and the dogmas of a religion will be the sole philosophic test which is available to us of the ethical validity of a religion. Assuming that the purpose of the conscience is to assist the principles of forward growth, and that assumption appears to me to be unavoidable, this test will show whether any particular religion is designed to assist the same process. The agreement of religion, it will be allowed, is of inestimable value. Without it, the most powerful among all the motives to human action will be left either unengaged or actively hostile. Human energy will either work at half time or be paralysed.

We have already seen that in the Kingdom of Heaven unselfishness to the point of complete self-repression and the extreme of undiluted humility are to reign. But nothing can be more certain than that no human community could continue to subsist for a day after it had completely attained this end: and the extent to which it could be reached by individuals may be liberally measured by a comparison of the total number of saints in a country with its total population. Without a very strong element of pride and competition no life could remain on earth; and morality, if left to itself, must stop short with a duality of final ends, and an equality of value between pride and humility. This, however it may appeal to metaphysics, is not what morality wants. The purpose of morality is guidance, and, when a man is in doubt between two roads, it is no use to tell him to follow both. The doctrine of the Church on earth tells him that while on earth he must follow both roads, but in such a way that humility shall always be his final end, and pride the means for attaining it. A comparison may, perhaps, be made with a tree, which at the same time throws its head towards the sky and pushes its roots into the ground. The latter, however, differs in having no conscience, and no conscious choice, to guide it.

That the government of the Church on earth admits no element of pride it would be absurd to assert. The Divine functions of the Head of the Roman Church invest him, both in his own opinion and that of the community over which he presides, with a dignity which is far above that of any temporal monarchy. In the Anglican Church the Archbishop ranks below the King and the Royal family, but above all other subjects. And the depth of the humility corresponds with the loftiness of the pride in each case. The Supreme Pontiff proclaims himself the servant of all the servants of God : the Archbishop does not give the same prominence to that title. What we have here is no compromise, no happy mean of Aristotle, but a steady simultaneous growth in opposite directions *ad infinitum* : and this is as far as the conscience, unaided, takes us.

The reason, reflecting on the phenomena of growth, discerns the need of a final end; but it is limited by the matter in which it moves. Philosophy cannot detach itself from its own experience, and, while it remains on earth, it can never deduce a single final end from a progression of opposites. It follows that many philosophers will content themselves by the assumption that the sign of growth has been a clear increase of happiness. Their definition of happiness will vary, and none has ever been discovered which either can be harmonized with the conscience or has been pursued without disaster. To set up a philosophic end means necessarily to discard the influences both of the conscience and of religion. The primitive curse on man is that by labour he shall eat his bread, and his first aim is to escape from that. His means are various. The merchant seeks ease and plenty through trade, the soldier by conquest; and both by making others bear the burden for them ; but none is successful. In the end, ' quisque suos patimur manes '.

The wise man, taught by repeated failures, will, like the Stoic, accept his doom on earth, but he will not, like him, stay at that point. If he did he would require all his pride and self-satisfaction to support him. Instead of that, One whom the Christians are agreed to revere as God has told us that we must seek our redemption in another world, and that our aim in this world is a complete withdrawal from its interests so far as they affect ourselves. But this duty does not imply indolence or neglect of the moral law. Man must still put forth all his powers in the interests of others, that is to say, of love, and, in that cause, must welcome even the bitterest humiliation. The only question left for him to decide is : what are the true interests of others? For the Jew, that question is answered by the law of Moses. The rule for the Christian must be universal and embrace all nations. It must everywhere be the conscience, but under the guidance of love. This solution is not obtained by the reason, nor does it receive any support from it. It is derived from revelation and accepted by faith. The reason, unaided, leads us to a dualism of two opposed ends. This, so far as truth is reasonable, is the truth. Why then do we hesitate to accept it? Because it fails to satisfy the purpose with which we sat down to reason; because it is useless. Let any one who doubts whether misery is not at least as real as happiness, or can take comfort from the silly philosophy that evil is merely a negation of good, read a good account of the late war. He will then be convinced of the reality of the burden, and may even be provoked to the madness of rebellion. But Christianity promises a release, and makes that, and no worldly aim, the final end of conduct on earth. By determining the direction which conduct on earth should take, it prescribes the conditions on which release from its burdens may be obtained.

A few words will suffice to sum up our conclusions as to the values, both philosophical and religious, of pleasure or pain, or happiness and misery, in the scheme of the world's progress. Both ethics and Christianity are indifferent, but in differing senses of that word; ethics because it has no data on which to form a judgement, Christianity because it judges earthly pains and pleasures as having no such importance as would entitle them to be taken into account. Ethics regards them both as necessary factors in the evolution of action, the function of pleasure being to stimulate, and of pain to control; and it concludes that both must always increase, at about an equal rate, throughout every period of forward evolution. It also shows that this has been the case during the history of the past; and that neither can be made a final end, whether to pursue or to avoid, without contradicting the conscience.

Christianity regards both as incidents in evolution, and therefore temporal and unreal, and not to be compared with the everlasting happiness or sufferings of a real existence after death. This gives rise to a freedom and elevation of spirit such as are not attainable under any other belief; to a detachment of character which is based not on despair but on faith, and on hope, and on love. It also gives us the assurance that any sacrifice we may make for the sake of the Kingdom will be repaid a hundredfold in this world.

The immeasurable distance in importance between the pleasures of earth and the bliss of Heaven tempts one to borrow the terms of metaphysics. But it is certain that the distinction between reality and appearance is purely Greek, and that it had no entry into, or effect upon, the theories of primitive Christianity. In nothing is this more evident than in the great value that was attached by the early Church to the doctrine of the resurrection of the body.

Good and evil, love and hatred, pleasure and pain are equally certain, and equally real, in this world and in the next. But in the next world there is no conflict; a great gulf is fixed between good and evil: here there is a conflict, and growth or decay,

CONCLUSION

and the need of a morality. To the Christian the distinction between real and unreal has no meaning. Everything is real when seen 'sub specie aeternitatis' and not otherwise. But nothing in this life can be known under that aspect; and the whole of our knowledge in all its phases, from the simplest perception to the most abstract generalization, is equally temporary.

PRINTED IN ENGLAND
AT THE OXFORD UNIVERSITY PRESS